Amazing
WOMEN

OVER 100 LIVES TO INSPIRE YOU

To all the amazing women in my life.
– LW

To my mom, a fellow amazing woman.
– SG

First American Edition 2018
Kane Miller, A Division of EDC Publishing

Text copyright © Lara Wilson and Stripes Publishing 2018
Illustrations copyright © Sarah Green 2018
First published in Great Britain in 2018 by Stripes Publishing,
an imprint of the Little Tiger Group.

For information contact:
Kane Miller, A Division of EDC Publishing
P.O. Box 470663
Tulsa, OK 74147-0663
www.kanemiller.com
www.edcpub.com
www.usbornebooksandmore.com

Library of Congress Control Number: 2017942428

Printed and bound in China

ISBN: 978-1-61067-735-6 (Flexi-bound)
ISBN: 978-1-61067-791-2 (American Library Binding)

Amazing WOMEN

OVER 100 LIVES TO INSPIRE YOU

Lara Wilson · Illustrated by Sarah Green

Kane Miller
A DIVISION OF EDC PUBLISHING

Contents

Introduction   7

INSPIRATION

Beyoncé   9
Maya Angelou   10
Jessica Ennis-Hill   10
Mother Teresa   11
Edith Cavell   12
Hillary Clinton   14
Josephine Baker   14
Delia Smith   15
Ellen DeGeneres   15
Malorie Blackman   16
Harper Lee   16
Michelle Obama   17
Irena Sendler   18
Billie Holiday   19
Hattie McDaniel   19
Nancy Reagan   20
Clara Barton   20
Julia Child   21
Audrey Hepburn   22
Margot Fonteyn   23
Madonna   23

TRAILBLAZER

Zaha Hadid   24
Danica Patrick   25
Hedy Larnarr   25
Kathryn Bigelow   26
Judy Blume   26
Margaret Thatcher   27
Katherine Johnson   28
Condoleezza Rice   30
Christa McAuliffe   30
Maria Tallchief   31
Rachel Carson   32
Benazir Bhutto   32
Billie Jean King   33
Junko Tabei   33
Martha Gellhorn   34
Shirin Ebadi   34

CAMPAIGNER

Temple Grandin   35
Rosa Parks   36
Tegla Loroupe   38
Germaine Greer   39
Helen Keller   39
Ayn Rand   40
Gloria Steinem   40

LEADER

Queen Elizabeth II   41
Melinda Gates   41
Eva Perón   42
Sheryl Sandberg   42
Laura Bush   43
Emmeline Pankhurst   44
Eleanor Roosevelt   46
Angela Merkel   46
Estée Lauder   47
Indira Gandhi   47
Kathleen Kennedy   48

PIONEER

Valentina Tereshkova   49
Carolyn Porco   49
Mary Leakey   50
Tu Youyou   50
Rosalind Franklin   51
Ann Bancroft   52
Maria Montessori   52
Radia Perlman   53
Marie Curie   53
Amelia Earhart   54
Inge Lehmann   56
Jane Cooke Wright   57
Zoe Sugg   57
Grace Murray Hopper   58

CREATOR

J.K. Rowling   59
Frida Kahlo   60
Virginia Woolf   62

Annie Leibovitz   62
Beatrix Potter   63
Lena Dunham   64
Judi Dench   64
Georgia O'Keeffe   65
Margaret Atwood   65
Lady Gaga   66
Elisabeth Lutyens   67
Sylvia Plath   67

ACTIVIST

Jaha Dukureh   68
Jeanne Manford   68
Jane Goodall   69
Nawal El Saadawi   70
Simone de Beauvoir   70
Constance Markievicz   71
Wangari Muta Maathai   71
Mairead Corrigan Maguire   72

VIRTUOSO

Aretha Franklin   74
Nicola Adams   74
Oprah Winfrey   75
Serena Williams   76
Meryl Streep   78
Agatha Christie   78
Björk   79
Coco Chanel   80
Florence Griffith Joyner   80
Joni Mitchell   81

YOUNG MOTIVATOR

Tavi Gevinson   82
Laura Dekker   82
Simone Biles   83
Anne Frank   84
Kiara Nirghin   85
Ellie Simmonds   85
Malala Yousafzai   86
You!   88

Glossary   91

Introduction

It is unimaginable to think that only one hundred years ago, life was strikingly different for women around the world. At the turn of the twentieth century, many women were still regarded as second-class citizens. We didn't have the right to vote. We faced obstacles to education and work. Our place was in the home, tending to the needs of our husbands and children, and we could only dream of one day becoming a doctor, a scientist, a lawyer or a politician.

It took a group of brave and bold suffragettes – women who fought for freedom and equal voting rights – to radically change the course of history for every female that followed. Led by the energetic Emmeline Pankhurst in the UK and other women like her around the world, the suffragette movement is one of the reasons why, in the twenty-first century, young women almost everywhere can dream big, aim high and achieve their ambitions.

Today women lead the charge in every field. Where would we be without the **Inspirations**, true icons who encourage us to achieve our wildest dreams? What about the **Trailblazers**, gutsy gals who risk life and limb to break new ground?

How about the **Campaigners**, heroes who give a voice to all those who, through prejudice and injustice, do not have one of their own? Life would be so very different without the **Leaders**, fierce females who challenge perceptions and dedicate their lives to breaking down barriers.

Then there are the **Pioneers**, women who, through their passion and curiosity, changed the world for the better. How dull life would be without the **Creators**, whose dedication to their craft knows no bounds! We also salute the **Activists**, women who have the courage to speak out for what they believe in. Through drive and determination, the **Virtuosos** have risen to the top of their field and are celebrated the world over. Finally let us not forget the **Young Motivators** – the champions, entrepreneurs and superstars of tomorrow.

Each of the women in this book has something in common – they are not afraid to stand out, speak up and work hard to accomplish their goals. They are the role models of the modern era. Now it is up to you to follow in their footsteps.

Beyoncé 1981–

Singer, Songwriter, Producer and Actor

Beyoncé is a megastar on a scale rarely seen before. Not only is she a powerhouse entertainer, global fashion icon and million-dollar business mogul, but she is also a wife, mother and humanitarian. Her entire career is an inspiration, her every move influential.

Beyoncé grew up in Texas. Her meteoric rise to the top began at seven, when she won her first talent contest. Soon after, she formed the girl group Girls Tyme, which became hit R&B band Destiny's Child. Through their many chart-topping anthems, the trio became one of the most popular female groups in history.

But it was when Beyoncé recorded her debut solo album, 2003's *Dangerously in Love*, that she transformed into the icon she is today. Featuring blockbuster single "Crazy in Love," the album won five GRAMMYs and catapulted the singer into the big time.

Since then, Beyoncé has been at the top of her game. Through sold-out world tours and incredible live performances with her all-female band Suga Mama, she showcases her sensational voice and masterful dancing. Her music videos are works of art, while the chart-topping "Single Ladies (Put a Ring on It)" became one of the best-selling singles of all time. In fact, Beyoncé had more US Top 10 singles than any other female artist in the 2000s! With 2016's *Lemonade*, she became the first artist in history to have their first six albums go to number one, and her staggering success shows no signs of stopping.

Beyoncé embodies strength, independence and female empowerment. She made curves cool again, is a savvy businesswoman and a role model to millions. All hail, Queen Bey!

"I'm over being a pop star. I don't wanna be a hot girl. I wanna be iconic."

Maya Angelou

1928–2014

Author, Poet and Civil Rights Activist

Her 1969 memoir, *I Know Why the Caged Bird Sings*, made history when it became the first nonfiction bestseller by an African-American woman. But when she died at eighty-six, Maya Angelou's legacy extended far beyond a single book.

Born in Missouri, Maya lived with her grandmother when her parents split up. But when she returned home at age seven, her mother's boyfriend attacked her. The trauma affected her so badly that she stopped speaking for five years. During this time of silence she found escape through poetry, eventually becoming a writer herself. She revealed her struggle to overcome racism and the events of her childhood through her books, essays and poems.

She also fought prejudice and organized marches during the Civil Rights movement. Through strength, wisdom and bravery, Maya has become an inspiration to millions facing difficulties in their own lives.

Jessica Ennis-Hill

1986–

Athlete

It was Super Saturday at the 2012 London Olympics. Jessica Ennis-Hill had just realized a lifelong dream, having triumphed in the heptathlon before an ecstatic home crowd.

On a day that saw twelve British golds, Jessica's victory was perhaps the most extraordinary. Having missed the competition four years earlier due to injury, in London she scored three personal bests and broke both the British and Commonwealth records! It was a long way from where it all began, in her hometown of Sheffield, UK, at a beginners' track and field event. Even then Jessica was a gifted all-around athlete, clearly made for the heptathlon – seven events of running, jumping and throwing, which test skill, stamina and speed.

With a string of medals to her name, Jessica is now a mother and retired from the sport. She was honored with a damehood in 2017.

Mother Teresa 1910–1997

Nun and Missionary

As a child, Anjezë Bojaxhiu believed it was her destiny to become a nun. At eighteen she left home to join the Sisters of Loreto in Ireland, before moving to India to teach at a convent. It was here that she chose her religious name, Mother Teresa, after the patron saint of missionaries, Thérèse de Lisieux.

While working at the convent in Kolkata, Mother Teresa witnessed terrible poverty and disease in the city's slums. In 1946, she said she received a message from God to leave the convent and dedicate her life to helping Kolkata's poor as a missionary. Those first years in the slums were fraught with difficulty – she had to beg for food and was often homeless herself, but soon the Catholic Church recognized her sacrifice, and in 1950, the Missionaries of Charity was born.

By 1996, the charity had grown to nearly 600 missions in over one hundred countries. Nobody was turned away: the nuns helped refugees, orphans, the sick and the dying. In her distinctive white sari with blue border, Mother Teresa traveled the world, assisting the survivors of earthquakes, famine and war.

Despite ill health, Mother Teresa carried on working until she was too sick to continue. In 1979, she was awarded the Nobel Peace Prize, and in 2016, she was recognized by the Catholic Church as a saint. One of history's greatest humanitarians, her lifelong compassion for the poorest people on Earth is a lesson to us all.

"Spread love everywhere you go. Let no one ever come to you without leaving happier."

Edith Cavell 1865-1915

Nurse

Between 1914 and 1918, the world was engaged in one of the bloodiest conflicts in history. Almost every major power took to the battlefield in World War I, leading to death and destruction on a massive scale. Much blood was spilled in the name of nationalism, but one courageous woman was determined to prevent politics from getting in the way of saving lives.

Edith Cavell was born in a village near Norfolk, UK. In her early twenties she worked as a teacher in the Sunday school at her father's church. Later she took a position as governess to a Belgian family. But when her father fell ill, she returned to England to care for him. It was then that she decided to train to become a nurse. Edith worked at several hospitals in England and was awarded a medal for her work during a particularly bad breakout of typhoid in Maidstone, Kent.

In 1907, Edith accepted the job of matron (head nurse) at the Berkendael Medical Institute in Brussels, Belgium. Up to that point, nuns had been caring for patients, despite little training. Edith was put in charge of training nurses and increasing the standards of Belgian healthcare. Such was her impact that she is now regarded as the founder of professional nursing in Belgium. But just four years later, everything would change.

When war broke out, Edith's nursing school in Belgium became a Red Cross hospital. During the German occupation of the country, she made it her mission to treat wounded soldiers from both sides of the conflict.

Despite the dangers, Edith began sheltering British, French and Belgian soldiers in the hospital. With the assistance of a secret network, she helped 200 men escape across the border to safety.

But she paid a high price for her bravery. On August 3, 1915, the German police arrested Edith on charges of treason. Several countries appealed for her freedom, but to no avail; Edith was sentenced to death by firing squad on the morning of October 12, 1915.

Although she had admitted her guilt, Edith's execution sparked international outrage. Thousands of men volunteered for the British Army upon hearing the news. Not long after, the United States entered the war, which eventually led to the Allied victory.

Edith received a state funeral at Westminster Abbey, an honor reserved for citizens who have made a significant contribution to their country. Today, a statue of Edith stands near London's Trafalgar Square in memory of the nurse who sacrificed her life for others.

"I realize that patriotism is not enough. I must have no hatred or bitterness towards anyone."

Hillary Clinton

1947–

Politician, First Lady and Secretary of State

Hillary Clinton has broken down more barriers than any other woman in US politics. After earning a degree from Yale Law School, she became one of the country's top lawyers. But when her husband was elected governor of Arkansas, Hillary decided to give her all to public life as Arkansas's First Lady. When Bill was elected president in 1992, she became the nation's First Lady and worked hard for women's equality and healthcare reform. Later, as secretary of state, she led diplomatic negotiations in the Middle East and promoted human rights.

In 2016, Hillary became the first woman in US history to run for president as a majority party's nominee. But despite winning the popular vote, she was defeated by Donald Trump, who won more electoral votes. Regardless of the election's outcome and her critics, Hillary remains a true role model to the female leaders of the future.

Josephine Baker

1906–1975

Dancer, Entertainer and Activist

Josephine Baker was one of the first African-Americans to become a stage and screen icon. Later, as a spy and civil rights activist, she became an inspiration to millions.

Born in Missouri, Josephine fled racial discrimination and moved to France, to further her dance career. There she electrified audiences with the exotic and athletic "Danse Sauvage" ("Wild Dance"), and performed in a skirt made from bananas alongside her pet cheetah Chiquita!

France had welcomed Josephine, and during World War II, she proved her loyalty to her adopted country by spying for the French Resistance. At the war's end, she received several of France's highest honors for her bravery!

Later, while touring the US, Josephine refused to perform to segregated audiences and became a figurehead of the Civil Rights movement until her death at sixty-nine. From sensational dancer to inspirational activist, Josephine was a heroine to the very end.

Delia Smith

1941–

Cook and Entrepreneur

Delia Smith is a world-class British cook, recipe writer and TV presenter. With her down-to-earth attitude she taught millions of kitchen novices how to boil an egg, bake the perfect sponge cake and turn out a festive turkey with all the trimmings. All this from a girl who left school without a single qualification.

Delia discovered her passion for food at age twenty-one. She was hired to write a newspaper cooking column, before moving on to presenting her TV cooking programs and releasing best-selling recipe books. Delia's second love is soccer – she is the majority shareholder of Norwich City Football Club, and was one of the first women to head a major professional team.

Today Delia runs her cooking empire from her website Delia Online, where her recipes continue to tantalize the taste buds of her fans.

Ellen DeGeneres

1958–

Comedian, Actor and Talk Show Host

As a comedian and TV host, Ellen DeGeneres brings joy to millions through her daytime talk show, *The Ellen DeGeneres Show*, which has entertained viewers since 2003.

As well as making people laugh for a living, in 1997 Ellen became one of the first celebrities to come out as a lesbian. Later that year, the TV character she played on *Ellen* also came out. This made Ellen the first openly lesbian actor to play an openly lesbian character on TV. She now devotes part of her life to supporting the LGBT community and striving for equality.

To some, Ellen is perhaps most famous as the voice of Dory in Pixar's *Finding Nemo* and *Finding Dory* films. She has also written four books, was named *Forbes'* fiftieth most powerful woman in the world in 2015 and has won more People's Choice awards than any other person! An inspiration to fans around the world, her humor, warmth and honesty make Ellen the people's favorite.

Malorie Blackman

1962–

Author and Screenwriter

Today, Malorie Blackman is a best-selling author of children's and young adult fiction and writer of popular TV programs. But when she was growing up in 1970s Britain, she often faced racial prejudice.

As a child, she struggled to find stories featuring black characters. Rather than allow these experiences to hold her back, Malorie used them to become an exceptional writer. In the series Noughts & Crosses, she tackles racism head-on by writing an alternative history, where the Noughts (black people) are in charge of the Crosses (white people).

Despite receiving over eighty rejection letters before her first book was published, Malorie overcame many barriers to become a successful author. In 2013, she became the UK's first black Children's Laureate, and through her writing she has inspired millions of teens.

Harper Lee

1926–2016

Author

Harper Lee's novel *To Kill a Mockingbird* (1960) is a classic. It tells the story of Tom Robinson, a black man who is accused of assaulting a white woman in the town of Maycomb, Alabama. This story of racial prejudice and injustice is told through the eyes of six-year-old Scout, as she learns how to determine right from wrong. Harper's novel reflects the turbulent events of the time in which she wrote it. During the 1960s, the Civil Rights movement saw violent protests, during which thousands marched for equal rights for African-Americans.

Despite her success, Harper stayed out of the spotlight. Instead, she chose to let *To Kill a Mockingbird* speak to the millions inspired by its themes of hope and peace during a time of deep division.

Michelle Obama 1964–

Lawyer and First Lady

Michelle Obama is a modern-day icon, known for her grace, warmth and dignity. As the first African-American First Lady, she was dedicated to changing the lives of those from disadvantaged backgrounds.

Michelle was always a high achiever. But in 1981, when she attended Princeton University, she faced racial discrimination on campus. However, through hard work and determination, Michelle overcame these barriers to graduate with honors and go on to Harvard Law School.

It was while working as a lawyer that she met Barack Obama, whom she married in 1992. After Barack decided to run for president, Michelle gave up work to support her husband on the campaign trail. Upon his election in 2008, Michelle turned her focus to social issues, such as poverty, health and equality. She visited homeless shelters, campaigned for women's and LGBT rights, and supported military families. She also started the campaign "Let's Move!" to tackle childhood obesity through healthy eating and fitness. Achieving all this while raising two daughters made her an inspiration to working mothers everywhere.

Michelle has truly made her mark on American history. She and Barack were clear on their mission during their time in the White House: they wanted to make a difference in people's lives, no matter their background, race or identity. There is little doubt we will see more of Michelle in the future.

"I never cut class... I loved getting As, I liked being smart. I liked being on time... I thought being smart was cooler than anything in the world."

Irena Sendler 1910–2008

Activist, Nurse and Social Worker

In September 1939, Germany invaded Poland, triggering World War II. Under orders from their leader, Adolf Hitler, German armed forces began rounding up Polish Jews and forcing them to live in ghettos.

Irena Sendler, a nurse and social worker in Poland's capital, Warsaw, began helping Jews to escape. She and several others faked thousands of documents to help Jewish families avoid detection. It was an immense act of bravery, since aiding Jews was punishable by death.

In 1943, Irena joined Zegota, an underground organization that secretly provided food, money and medicine to Jews in hiding. With Zegota's help, Irena smuggled babies and children out of the ghettos to safety. She kept records of the children's identities so that they could be reunited with their families at the end of the war. In this way, Irena saved 2,500 children from certain death.

However, the Gestapo (Nazi secret police) finally caught up with Irena. They arrested and tortured her, but she never gave up the names of her helpers or the children she saved. She was sentenced to execution, but escaped when Zegota bribed her guards.

Finally, when the war ended, Irena gathered the children's documents and prepared to reunite them with their families, but nearly all the parents had died in the concentration camps.

Irena saved more Jews than any other person during the war. She received many honors for her heroism, including Poland's highest civilian medal, the Order of the White Eagle. Before she died at age ninety-eight, she was able to reunite with many of the children she had saved.

"Heroes do extraordinary things. What I did was not an extraordinary thing. It was normal."

Billie Holiday

1915–1959

Singer

The stage lights darken in the tiny nightclub. A spotlight illuminates the white gardenias in the singer's hair. For an unknown with no musical training, Billie Holiday's performance is spellbinding. Soon she would become one of the greatest jazz vocalists of all time.

Billie grew up in extreme poverty during a time of deep segregation, but she found comfort in music and began singing in New York's nightclubs. Her unique style quickly made her one of the swing era's stars, and she was among the first black singers to perform with an all-white orchestra. However, she experienced poisonous racism at her shows. These encounters led her to "Strange Fruit," a harrowing song about a black man's lynching. Though controversial, the powerful song is considered Billie's masterpiece.

Billie's talent brought success, but her life was one of pain. She lost her battle with substance abuse at just forty-four, yet her haunting voice will live forever.

Hattie McDaniel

1895–1952

Actor and Singer

Hattie McDaniel blazed a trail for black stage and screen stars: she was the first African-American to win an Oscar and the first black woman to sing on US radio. Yet she faced racism throughout her career.

Born in Kansas to former slaves, Hattie loved to sing and got her big break on radio in the 1920s. Later, despite tough competition, she won the role of the maid "Mammy" in the epic film *Gone with the Wind*. It earned her the Best Supporting Actress Oscar in 1939, but segregation laws stopped her from attending the film's premiere. Some civil rights groups also criticized her for contributing to the stereotype that black actors could only play servants.

Hattie died in 1952, but segregation also prevented her burial alongside other movie stars at Hollywood Forever Cemetery. Her work was finally recognized in 1975 with her induction into the Black Filmmakers Hall of Fame.

Nancy Reagan

1921–2016

First Lady and Actor

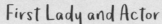

Nancy Reagan played a number of movie roles, but she is best known for being the 40th First Lady of the United States. She met Ronald Reagan, then a fellow actor, when he was president of the Screen Actors Guild, and they married in 1952. As he embarked on a political career, the pair left Hollywood behind them.

When Ronald Reagan became president in 1981, Nancy was determined to bring her style and influence to the White House. She also soon became known for her charitable work. She was a keen supporter of the Girl Scouts and was responsible for the "Just Say No" drug education campaign.

In her later years, after her husband was diagnosed with Alzheimer's, she became actively involved with the National Alzheimer's Association. Nancy campaigned tirelessly for stem cell research, in the hope that science could one day lead to a cure for the disease.

Clara Barton

1821–1912

Founder of the American Red Cross

When the Civil War broke out in 1861, Clara Barton was working in Washington, D.C. Although she had no formal medical training, she left her job to tend to wounded soldiers. She risked her life, becoming known as the "Angel of the Battlefield." This was the start of Clara's career of helping people in times of conflict and disaster.

After the war, Clara traveled to Europe where she learned about the work of the International Red Cross. She was determined to bring the organization to her home country and, in 1881, the American Red Cross was founded. Clara was its president for twenty-three years, aiding with natural disasters, and helping the poor and homeless.

At the age of ninety, she died at her home in Glen Echo, Maryland. In 1974, it was designated as a National Historic Site, the first dedicated to the achievements of a woman.

Julia Child 1912–2004

Chef, author and television personality

Julia Child was an early celebrity TV chef. With her passion for French cuisine, she changed the way the American public cooked, ate and thought about food. She presented prime-time cooking shows for over forty years and wrote numerous cookbooks. Her memoir about her life in France became the basis for the hit film *Julie & Julia*.

But Julia was not always a master chef, and she could hardly speak any French when she moved to Paris with her diplomat husband at the age of thirty-six. Falling in love with French food, she signed up to attend the exclusive Cordon Bleu cooking school and was the only woman on her professional course. She went on to set up a cooking school, with Simone Beck and Louisette Bertholle, and together they began work on *Mastering the Art of French Cooking*. The idea behind the book was simple – to introduce Americans to classic French dishes by making the recipes as accessible as possible. It took ten years to write and contained 524 recipes, providing detailed step-by-step instructions and lists of ingredients readers might find in their local supermarket.

To publicize the book Julia cooked an omelet on live TV, and was then approached to present her first series, *The French Chef*. On-screen, she came across as both informative and approachable. Her easygoing humor when she dropped a pan or spilled a sauce quickly gained her a legion of fans.

Julia's cooking shows won many broadcasting awards, including several Emmys. In 2000, she was awarded the Legion of Honour by the French government. Even after her death, Julia continues to inspire and motivate food lovers through her Foundation for Gastronomy and the Culinary Arts.

"Find something you're passionate about and keep tremendously interested in it."

Audrey Hepburn 1929–1993

Actor and Activist

Audrey Hepburn was an international movie star and a style icon, known for her grace and beauty. But it was her work offscreen as an ambassador to the world's poorest people that made her an inspiration.

Audrey grew up in Belgium and the Netherlands during World War II, but eventually moved to London to study ballet and become an actor. Her big break came when she was cast as Princess Ann in the film *Roman Holiday* in 1953. Despite being a virtual unknown, she became the first woman to win a BAFTA, Oscar and Golden Globe for Best Actress for a single role.

In 1961, Audrey charmed the world as Holly Golightly in *Breakfast At Tiffany's*, a role that made her a screen legend. With her short dark hair, slender figure and full eyebrows, she represented a new type of feminine beauty not seen before in Hollywood. This made her an inspiration to top fashion designers and young women hoping to copy her distinctive look.

Later, remembering the terrible experiences she faced growing up during the war, Audrey dedicated her life to humanitarian causes. She was appointed a UNICEF International Goodwill Ambassador and toured the poorest parts of Africa, Asia and South America, assisting those in need of food, shelter, clean water and vaccinations.

In 1992, Audrey was awarded the Presidential Medal of Freedom for her humanitarian work. Sadly, she died the following year, a heroine of the silver screen who had become a real-life heroine to millions around the world.

"Nothing is impossible, the word itself says 'I'm possible'!"

Margot Fonteyn

1919–1991

Ballerina

Margot Fonteyn was an icon of British ballet with a glittering career. Her charm, glamour and grace made her one of the most cherished dancers of all time.

At just four, Margot's mother enrolled her in ballet classes, and by fourteen she had joined the Vic-Wells Ballet School (now known as the Royal Ballet). There, Margot made her debut as a snowflake in *The Nutcracker*, but was soon cast in every principal role, from *The Sleeping Beauty* to *Swan Lake*. By 1939, she was appointed *prima ballerina assoluta*, a rare honor awarded to the most remarkably talented female dancer in the ballet company. With dance partners Robert Helpmann and Rudolf Nureyev, she performed to packed houses and received hundreds of encores!

Margot was never a flashy dancer; rather, perfection, simplicity and symmetry were her strengths. A true professional with a magical stage presence, she will always be remembered as a master of her craft.

Madonna

1958–

Singer and Songwriter

Madonna is so much more than a pop star. A pioneer, revolutionary and rebel, her over thirty-year career at the top of the charts has made her a living legend and global icon.

Madonna Louise Ciccone grew up in Michigan before moving to New York, where she eventually got her big break with Sire Records. Since then, she has sold more than 300 million records, making her the best-selling female artist of all time! Many of her hit songs, such as "Like A Prayer," "Express Yourself" and "Vogue," are among the most iconic in music history. She is also never afraid to speak her mind; she battles sexism and ageism, and has spearheaded campaigns for women's equality, HIV/AIDS and LGBT rights.

Madonna has shocked, entertained and evolved into one of the most fascinating performers of all time. Fearless, fierce and fabulous, she is truly the undisputed "Queen of Pop"!

Zaha Hadid 1950–2016

Architect

Zaha Hadid was a trailblazer in more ways than one. As a world-famous architect, she was the first woman, and first Iraqi, to win both the Pritzker Architecture Prize and the Royal Institute of British Architects Gold Medal. But as a hugely successful female in a male-dominated profession, she was an inspiration to women around the world.

Born in Iraq, Zaha moved to London in 1972 to study architecture. Even then, her visionary talent stood out, and she won many competitions with her innovative paintings and sketches. Eventually, in 1993, she got her first commission – to build the Vitra Fire Station in Germany. The radical design – all glass, concrete and curves – won her instant fans and more projects around the world.

Zaha went on to design some of the most daring and inventive buildings and bridges ever seen. Her work had one focus: to avoid ninety-degree angles, leading to her nickname, "Queen of the Curve." The Sheikh Zayed Bridge, which connects Abu Dhabi to Dubai, is shaped like a giant sweeping wave, while the Guangzhou Opera House in China resembles two enormous smooth pebbles wrapped in granite and glass.

In the UK, Zaha's adopted country, she designed the Riverside Museum in Glasgow, with its mountain-peaked roof. She also created the London Aquatics Centre for the water-based events in the 2012 London Olympics, its flowing outline simulating water in motion.

Zaha was celebrated throughout her life and was made a dame in 2012 for her contribution to architecture. A force of nature, she fought hard for her place as one of the greatest architects in history.

"I am sure that as a woman I can do a very good skyscraper."

Danica Patrick

1982–

Race Car Driver

Motorsports are exhilarating, but collisions are unavoidable at breakneck speeds of 200 miles per hour. However, one determined female took on the challenge of this male-dominated discipline and changed open-wheel racing forever.

Danica Patrick was ten when she started go-karting. By 2008, she was the first woman to win an Indy race. She also holds the record for consecutive races finished running in the 2010 season (thirty-three).

Next Danica took on stock-car racing, becoming the first female to win a NASCAR pole position, with the fastest qualifying lap for the Daytona 500 in decades – an electrifying 45.817 seconds! However, during the 2016 NASCAR Sprint Cup at Talladega, she got into "the worst [wreck] of her career" when she collided with a wall, and her car caught fire.

But Danica was soon back on track and in the driver's seat, inspiring women everywhere. As she says, "I was brought up to be the fastest *driver*, not the fastest girl."

Hedy Lamarr

1914–2000

Actor and Inventor

When Austrian Hedy Lamarr moved to Hollywood to pursue an acting career, she became famous for her exotic beauty. But she soon tired of the lack of challenging roles and meaningful scripts, and so she took up inventing.

During World War II, Hedy realized that the enemy could interfere with communication signals that guided radio-controlled torpedoes. With composer George Antheil, she invented a system that spread the signals across different frequencies, making it nearly impossible for the enemy to divert a torpedo off course.

However, limited technology at the time prevented the invention from being used in the war. Finally in 1962, an updated version of Hedy's "Secret Communications System" was installed on US Navy ships, and today her work is essential to both Wi-Fi and Bluetooth technology. At long last, she had proved that she was so much more than just a pretty face.

Kathryn Bigelow

1951–

Film Director, Producer and Writer

Kathryn Bigelow made history in 2010 when she became the first woman to win the Oscar for Best Director. To date she is the only woman to win the award, but she is hopeful this will change.

Born in California, Kathryn studied filmmaking at Columbia University. She quickly went from making short movies to directing. With the movies *Point Break* (1991) and *Strange Days* (1995), Kathryn developed her style of fast-paced action and gripping stories.

In 2008, Kathryn directed a tense thriller about an American bomb disposal unit working in Iraq during the war. *The Hurt Locker* was so powerful that many critics named it the best film of the year. Not only did Kathryn win the Academy Award for Best Director, but the film also won a further five awards, including Best Picture, making Kathryn one of today's most sought-after directors.

Judy Blume

1938–

Author and Activist

For preteen book lovers, writer Judy Blume is something of a hero. Her coming-of-age stories, including *Are You There God? It's Me, Margaret* (1970), *It's Not the End of the World* (1972) and *Blubber* (1974), tackle such tricky topics as divorce, bullying and puberty. At a time when many people thought these subjects inappropriate for children's books, Judy's sensitive stories helped millions of readers. But her books were banned in schools and some libraries. Never one to give in to the critics, Judy joined the National Coalition Against Censorship to fight for freedom in reading and writing.

Judy's books have since sold 82 million copies worldwide. Despite falling ill with cancer, she continues to speak out against censorship and create characters that are a source of comfort to young adults around the world.

Margaret Thatcher 1925–2013

Politician and Prime Minister

Margaret Thatcher was a formidable woman and a political pioneer. The first female British prime minister, she led the country from 1979 to 1990, and became one of the most significant world leaders of the twentieth century.

After studying chemistry at Oxford University, Margaret first became a research chemist, but she was also drawn to politics. In her twenties, she joined the Conservative party and ran in (but lost) several local elections. During this time she met and married Denis Thatcher and took a break from politics to become a barrister before giving birth to twins. Finally, in 1959, Margaret was elected as a member of parliament for Finchley, and her journey to the top began.

Throughout the 1960s and 1970s, Margaret rose through the ranks of the Conservative party, until she was voted party leader in 1975. At the time, the UK's economy was extremely weak, with millions unemployed. Margaret seized her chance and stormed to victory in the 1979 general election.

With strong principles and firm policies, Margaret's leadership was divisive. During her three terms as prime minister, many saw her as an enemy of the working class and trade unions, while others hailed her as a hero for strengthening the UK economy and standing up to the might of the communist Soviet Union, leading to her nickname, "the Iron Lady."

But there is no doubting Margaret's impact on history. The longest-serving British prime minister to date, she restored faith in the UK economy, led the country through war and the threat of terrorism, and had a hugely influential impact on global politics.

> "I've got a woman's ability to stick to a job and get on with it when everyone else walks off and leaves it."

Katherine Johnson 1918–

Physicist and Mathematician

To the world, Katherine Johnson is known as the "Human Computer." Through her work on NASA space missions, she helped to catapult US astronauts into space, despite living and working in a time of segregation.

Katherine was born in West Virginia and showed a talent for math from a young age. But as an African-American growing up in the Deep South during the 1930s, she faced severe racism. The local high school didn't accept black students, so Katherine attended school in another town. She excelled and went on to earn degrees in both math and French at only eighteen. She hoped to study for her master's degree at West Virginia University, but once again, segregation threatened to hold her back. However, in a historic court case in 1939, the US Supreme Court ruled to desegregate the all-white university. Katherine became one of just three African-American students – and the only girl – selected to attend, and she enrolled in every math class she could. Her life as a mathematician had finally begun.

In 1953, Katherine joined NASA's Guidance and Navigation Department. There, along with a group of African-American women including Dorothy Vaughan and Mary Jackson, Katherine read data and performed complex mathematical tasks. She still faced racial and gender barriers, but her brilliant mind led to her calculating the flight path for a momentous journey: the first American manned mission into space. On May 5, 1961, astronaut Alan Shepard left Earth's atmosphere on the Project Mercury's *Freedom 7* spacecraft, which splashed safely into the Atlantic Ocean some fifteen minutes later. The mission was declared a success!

Katherine continued to calculate launch windows for space flights and plotted back-up plans in case of failure. In 1962, when NASA first began using computers, astronaut John Glenn insisted that Katherine check the computers' calculations for his orbit around Earth, such was her talent!

In 1969, Katherine was faced with her most important task to date: to calculate the flight path for the Apollo 11 mission to the Moon.

As Neil Armstrong set foot on the Moon's dusty surface – the first person ever to do so – Katherine watched the live footage with a mixture of pride and relief. The United States had won the "space race" and Katherine had played a huge part in the historic mission's success. A year later, when the Apollo 13 flight ran into difficulties, it was Katherine's backup procedures that helped save the crew and return them safely to Earth.

In 2015, Katherine was finally recognized for her work – she was awarded the Presidential Medal of Freedom, and NASA opened the Katherine G. Johnson Computational Research Facility in her honor. She and her colleagues were also the subject of the award-winning 2016 film, *Hidden Figures*, which celebrates their historic achievements.

"I counted the steps to the road, the steps up to church, the number of dishes and silverware I washed ... anything that could be counted, I did."

Condoleezza Rice

1954–

Secretary of State

As the first female African-American Secretary of State, Condoleezza Rice was in charge of foreign policy from 2005 to 2009. Before that, she was President George W. Bush's National Security Advisor – the first woman to occupy that post. *Forbes* magazine described her as the most powerful woman in the world and she appeared on *Time* magazine's list of the world's 100 most influential people four times.

Growing up in the Deep South when it was still segregated, Condoleezza was taught that to succeed she would need to be "twice as good" as non-minorities. She took this lesson to heart, starting college at just 15, and learning French and classical piano alongside her studies.

Condoleezza now lectures in politics and business at Stanford University, and has also written a number of bestselling books. She was a sometimes controversial figure during her political career, but her legacy is undeniable.

Christa McAuliffe

1948–1986

Teacher

On January 20, 1986, people across the US watched the launch of the Space Shuttle *Challenger*. Tragically, less than two minutes into its flight, the ship broke up over the Atlantic Ocean, killing everyone on board. Among the seven crew was high school teacher Christa McAuliffe.

Both the first American woman and the first African-American in space had previously flown aboard the *Challenger*, and Christa was set to follow in their historic footsteps as the first ordinary American in space. She had been selected from more than 11,000 applicants for NASA's Teacher in Space Project. She passionately wanted to help students better understand space and had gone through months of intensive training.

After her death, schools were named in Christa's honor, as well as an asteroid and a crater on the moon. In 2004, she was awarded the Congressional Space Medal of Honor for her extreme sacrifice in the name of space exploration.

Maria Tallchief

1925–2013

Ballerina

Maria Tallchief was born in Oklahoma in 1925 on the Osage Indian reservation. Not only did she go on to become the first Native American prima ballerina, but she was a pioneer of American ballet. At a time when the field was dominated by Russian and European dancers, she was the first American to perform both with the Paris Opera Ballet and on the stage of Moscow's Bolshoi Theater.

But although her talent for dance was clear from an early age, her early on-stage experiences were less positive. As children, she and her sister Marjorie, who also became a celebrated ballerina, were asked to dress up to perform "tribal" dance routines at country fairs. She later described these as *not* "remotely authentic" – traditionally, women didn't dance in Indian tribal ceremonies. They were both relieved when they outgrew their costumes.

When she was seventeen she moved to New York to pursue her dream of becoming a ballerina and joined the famous Ballet Russe de Monte Carlo. But while friends encouraged her to adopt a Russian stage name, as many American dancers did at the time, she was proud of her Indian heritage and refused.

Here she met legendary choreographer George Balanchine. When he cofounded what is now known as the New York City Ballet in 1946, Maria became the company's first star. Inspired by Maria's speed, athleticism, and passion, Balanchine created many striking and technically demanding roles for her. These included her signature role as the lead in *Firebird*.

"Above all, I wanted to be appreciated as a prima ballerina who happened to be a Native American..."

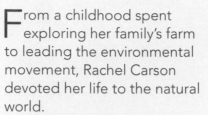

Rachel Carson
1907–1964

Marine Biologist, Conservationist and Author

From a childhood spent exploring her family's farm to leading the environmental movement, Rachel Carson devoted her life to the natural world.

After studying marine biology and zoology, Rachel became only the second woman to work for the Bureau of Fisheries. There, she was chief editor of science publications and wrote her first book, *The Sea Around Us*, a best-selling "biography of the sea." But it was her 1962 book, *Silent Spring*, that made her the voice of the new "green" movement. In it she warned of the harmful effects of DDT pesticides on the environment. Chemical companies fiercely opposed Rachel's findings, but her work led to a nationwide ban on DDT and the creation of the Environmental Protection Agency.

At fifty-six, Rachel succumbed to cancer. She was posthumously awarded the Presidential Medal of Freedom in 1980 for helping to preserve the environment for generations to come.

Benazir Bhutto
1953–2007

Politician and Prime Minister

Benazir Bhutto was Pakistan's eleventh prime minister and the first woman to lead a Muslim nation.

Benazir was educated in the West, which she said helped to form her belief in democracy. Her father was prime minister of Pakistan, and she grew up surrounded by politics. But it was after a military coup overthrew his government and killed him by hanging that Benazir sprang into action. She helped form the Movement for the Restoration of Democracy to challenge the military's rule and later was elected twice as prime minister.

Benazir was assassinated in 2007 while leaving a campaign rally. She was a controversial and often divisive figure, but many regard Benazir as a trailblazer who paved the way for more Muslim women to take on powerful public roles.

Billie Jean King

1943–

Tennis Player and Equal Rights Activist

Billie Jean King is as celebrated for her achievements off the tennis court as she is for her victories on it. She championed the rights of female tennis players at a time when gender equality was limited. When she won the US Open in 1972, she received $15,000 less than the male champion. Billie decided to take a stand: she refused to play the following year if things didn't change. The tennis world listened – in 1973, the US Open was the first tournament to award equal prize money. During the "Battle of the Sexes," Billie also beat retired professional Bobby Riggs in a promotional match that brought more fans to women's tennis.

Aside from her thirty-nine Grand Slam titles, Billie is also the founder of the Women's Tennis Association and was the first openly gay female athlete. Without her brave battle for equality, the world of professional women's tennis would look very different today.

Junko Tabei

1939–2016

Mountaineer

Junko Tabei became fascinated with mountains on a school trip to Mount Nasu, Japan, but it wasn't until she formed the Ladies' Climbing Club in 1969 that she started planning serious expeditions. By 1972, she was famed for climbing, but her toughest challenge was yet to come.

At a dizzying 29,029 feet above sea level, Mount Everest is the tallest peak on Earth. Junko was determined to conquer it. In 1975, she and a group of fifteen, mostly women, traveled to Kathmandu to attempt the ascent. Disaster struck when an avalanche hit their campsite at 20,669 feet, leaving Tabei buried underneath the snow and fighting for oxygen, until her Sherpa saved her life. Most would have called off the challenge right there, but twelve days later, Junko became the first woman to summit Everest.

Martha Gellhorn

1908–1998

Writer and Journalist

Very few would volunteer to go into a war zone, but journalist Martha Gellhorn's determination to report from the front lines saw her travel to almost every major battlefield in her lifetime. Martha's career began when she documented the Great Depression's impact on poor families in rural America. During World War II she journeyed to front lines across Europe and Asia. On D-day, when brutal battles killed tens of thousands of Allied and German troops, Martha was the only woman to land on the French beaches, after stowing away on a hospital ship! She also rode with British pilots on bombing raids over Germany.

In her eighties, failing eyesight put an end to Martha's work, but she will always be remembered for revealing to the world the struggles of ordinary people living through extraordinary times.

Shirin Ebadi

1947–

Lawyer, Judge and Human Rights Activist

Shirin Ebadi was one of the first female judges and the first female Chief Justice in Iran. But in the 1970s and 1980s, women were forbidden from practicing law in the country, and it wasn't until 1993 that Shirin could return to her work.

Since then she has become famous for defending people accused of various crimes in her home country, while her campaigns led to the creation of an Iranian law that protects children.

In 2003, and in recognition of her efforts in the fight for human rights, Shirin became the first-ever Iranian, and the first Muslim woman, to win the Nobel Peace Prize. She and five other female Nobel peace laureates went on to found the Nobel Women's Initiative in 2006. The global organization aims to unite women around the world in their support for world peace, justice and equality.

Temple Grandin 1947–

Animal Welfare Consultant, Autism Spokesperson and Professor of Animal Science

Temple Grandin is an expert on livestock behavior and treatment. She also has autism, and her unique mind enables her to relate to farm animals and improve their quality of life.

Temple didn't speak until she was nearly four years old, and she shied away from human contact. At the time, autism wasn't properly understood, and doctors recommended that she live in a mental-health facility. But Temple's mother fought against this, and her daughter attended public school.

Temple found school life difficult; she was bullied for her repetitive speaking and reactions to loud noise. But she was determined to succeed and went on to earn degrees in psychology and animal science, finding her calling in fighting for the humane treatment of animals in slaughterhouses and on farms. Her autism allowed her to spot needed improvements that others overlooked. Cows react badly to loud noises in their environment, so Temple pushed for dangling chains and banging gates to be removed. She also invented curved corrals, which reduce the animals' anxiety, and a scoring system to assess animal welfare. Now her facilities house almost half of the cattle in the United States!

Today Temple is a professor of animal science at Colorado State University and a world-famous speaker on autism. She has written several best-selling books, and in 2016, was inducted into the American Academy of Arts and Sciences.

"If I could snap my fingers and be non-autistic, I would not... Autism is part of who I am."

Rosa Parks 1913–2005

Civil Rights Activist

Only a generation ago, black people in the US were banned from going to many of the same places as white people. They were not allowed to drink from the same water fountains or eat at the same diners. They were sent to segregated schools and barred from taking certain jobs. They were also forced to give up their seats on busy buses to white people.

Rosa Parks grew up in Alabama during this time of widespread segregation. She had faced racism in all its cruelest forms since childhood, and in later life joined the National Association for the Advancement of Colored People (NAACP) to fight for civil rights. Progress was slow, and on December 1, 1955, Rosa decided she could no longer stand aside.

After a long day of work, Rosa boarded a bus to go home. She took a seat in a row reserved for black people. But when the bus filled up, the driver commanded Rosa to surrender her seat to a white person. Tired of giving in, Rosa refused; she was willing to risk the consequences to fight for her right to remain seated. Minutes later, police arrested Rosa, and she was charged with disorderly conduct for violating segregation laws. It was a defiant moment in one woman's life, but this simple act would go on to change the entire country.

The NAACP quickly rallied around Rosa and planned to boycott the Montgomery Bus Association. On the day of Rosa's trial, over 40,000 black people stopped using public transportation. Days later, the Montgomery Improvement Association was formed in order to continue the fight against city segregation laws. The group voted a young minister as their president. His name was Dr. Martin Luther King, Jr.

Just over a year later, and with the ongoing bus boycott draining city finances, Montgomery's buses were desegregated. Rosa's refusal to move from her seat became a symbol of the fight for equality and galvanized the Civil Rights movement, under King's strong leadership. But Rosa suffered for her courage – she lost her job and she and her husband had to leave Montgomery, after which they moved to Michigan. There Rosa got a job with a congressman, and through her work, continued campaigning for black welfare, housing and education rights.

Rosa's bravery led to her being named the "Mother of the Civil Rights movement." Throughout her life she received many of the nation's highest honors, including the Spingarn Medal, the Presidential Medal of Freedom and the Congressional Gold Medal. Upon her death, Rosa became the first woman and only the second African-American to lie in state in the Capitol Building, a rare honor usually reserved for presidents and statesmen. She proved that it takes just one person to inspire a revolution.

"I would like to be remembered as a person who wanted to be free ... so other people would also be free."

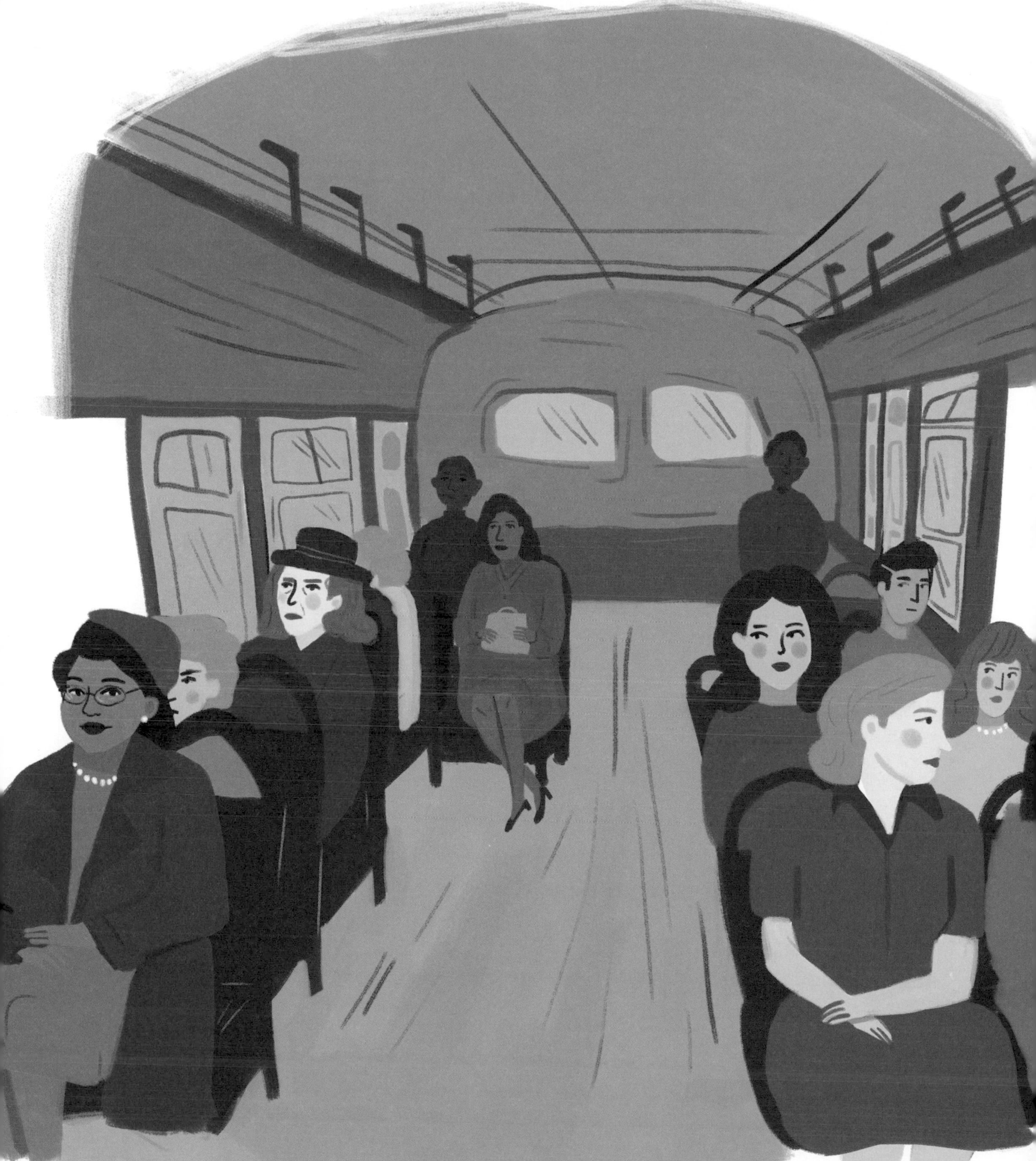

Tegla Loroupe 1973-

Athlete and Peace Activist

Growing up in a country famed for its male long-distance runners, Tegla Loroupe wondered whether her dream of joining them on the winner's podium would come to pass. However, at just twenty-one, she became the first African woman to win a major marathon (in New York City) and an idol to young women in her homeland of Kenya.

One of twenty-four siblings (her father had four wives), Tegla lived in a rural village and had to run over six miles to and from school every day. When she realized she could run faster than older students, she decided to become a professional.

After she started training with Athletics Kenya, she was soon winning medals in top races, including the Rotterdam, Berlin and London marathons. Often she would run barefoot, just as she had at home!

But Tegla is much more than a supreme athlete. Through the Tegla Loroupe Peace Foundation, she uses her sport to bring peace to war-torn countries. In 2003, she created the annual Peace Marathon, which sees government leaders, officials and local tribal warriors compete against each other to promote friendship. She also organized the Refugee Team for the 2016 Rio Olympics. This united displaced athletes from across Africa and the Middle East to compete as one team for the first time in Olympic history.

Next up for Tegla is the expansion of her Peace Academy, which provides education to children who have lost their parents to violence and disease. Through Tegla's passion and commitment, her race for peace is out of the starting blocks and heading for victory.

"One must be one's own inspiration."

Germaine Greer

1939–

Writer and Feminist

Germaine Greer has been at the forefront of the feminist movement ever since she published her first book, *The Female Eunuch*, in 1970. In it she declared that women are taught from a young age to be subservient to men and to conform to male ideals of what a woman should be. The book was controversial, but it became an instant bestseller and was translated into eleven languages!

Germaine became the figurehead of a type of feminism known as "women's liberation," which she believed meant that women should not aim for equality with men but rather fight for their own distinct identities. She also called for society to change from a patriarchy (run by men, for men) to one that would suit both genders.

Since *The Female Eunuch* was published, women and society have come a long way, but Germaine's book remains a landmark of the feminist movement.

Helen Keller

1880–1968

Author, Lecturer and Activist

Helen Keller is an idol to millions of people. Born in Alabama, she fell ill at nineteen months, losing both her sight and hearing. Helen communicated with her family through her own form of sign language. Later she met Anne Sullivan at the Perkins Institute for the Blind. Anne taught Helen to communicate by spelling words into her hand. It was a long, frustrating process, but at twenty-four Helen made history as the first deaf-blind person to earn a college degree!

She then learned to speak and read Braille, becoming a world-famous lecturer, author and activist.

In 1915, Helen began the Helen Keller International Organization, and later played a role in founding the ACLU. She was eventually awarded the Presidential Medal of Freedom, having proved to the world that with hard work and determination, blind-deaf people are just as capable as everyone else.

Ayn Rand

1905–1982

Writer and Philosopher

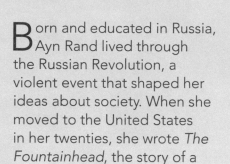

Born and educated in Russia, Ayn Rand lived through the Russian Revolution, a violent event that shaped her ideas about society. When she moved to the United States in her twenties, she wrote *The Fountainhead*, the story of a young architect who struggles against the establishment.

In *Atlas Shrugged* (1957), Ayn developed her political theory of "objectivism." It states that capitalism is the best form of government, as it recognizes individual rights and limits government control. In this system, people have the right to make their own choices and better themselves through hard work.

Ayn's ideas still attract both praise and fierce criticism. Many on the political left argue that capitalism promotes greed and selfishness. However, to many on the political right, Ayn is a hero and her theory of objectivism is "a philosophy for living on Earth."

Gloria Steinem

1934–

Journalist and Feminist

As a child, Gloria Steinem witnessed her mother suffer a nervous breakdown and struggle to keep a job. She saw this as the result of an "anti-female" society, in which women faced social and political inequality, and decided to act.

In 1972, she cofounded the magazine *Ms.*, which became a symbol of the feminist movement. Gloria is also pro-choice (the belief that women should have the right to choose to have children or not) and is a founder of the National Women's Political Caucus (NWPC), which helps women to get into political office. At the NWPC's first meeting, Gloria delivered the landmark speech, "Address to the Women of America," in which she said we must all strive for a society free of sexism.

In 2013, Gloria received the Presidential Medal of Freedom, and she continues to inspire women all over the world to fight for equality.

Queen Elizabeth II

1926–

Monarch

June 2, 1953. Twenty-five-year-old Elizabeth Windsor walks the central aisle at Westminster Abbey in full royal regalia. That day, to the cheers of thousands, she would be crowned Queen Elizabeth II, head of the UK and Commonwealth.

Thrust into the position when her father, George VI, died, the queen has since devoted her life to public service. In 2015, she became the world's longest-ever reigning monarch, ruling through changes to the British constitution, wars involving her subjects, and the governments of 160 prime ministers! The queen and her husband, the Duke of Edinburgh, are also patrons to over 1,000 charities. Now in her nineties, Queen Elizabeth II still works tirelessly to fulfill the duties of her coronation oath.

Melinda Gates

1964–

Businesswoman and Philanthropist

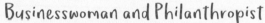

Melinda Gates was fascinated by computers from a young age. After earning a degree in computer science and economics, she got her first job in 1987, at Microsoft. There, she worked her way up to Microsoft General Manager of Information Products and also met and married Microsoft cofounder, Bill Gates.

The husband and wife team – the world's richest couple – later formed the Bill & Melinda Gates Foundation. They have since donated an incredible $30 billion to developments in global health and education. The foundation funds studies into malaria, tuberculosis and HIV/AIDS treatments, and delivers vaccines to hundreds of millions in developing countries. It also provides underprivileged minorities in the United States with the funds and support to access higher education.

Bill and Melinda's charity has saved or changed the lives of billions, but they're not stopping yet – they are fully committed to their vision of opportunity for all.

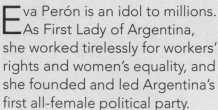

Eva Perón

First Lady

Eva Perón is an idol to millions. As First Lady of Argentina, she worked tirelessly for workers' rights and women's equality, and she founded and led Argentina's first all-female political party.

Growing up in poverty, at fifteen Eva fled to Buenos Aires to pursue her dream of becoming an actor. But there she met and married Juan Perón, and her life changed overnight. When Juan was elected president in 1946, Eva became First Lady. She quickly gained the adoration of the working classes, whom she encouraged to call her "Evita" (Little Eva). Through the Eva Perón Foundation she distributed shoes and cooking pots to the poor and needy, many of whom thought of her as a modern-day saint.

Tragically, at just thirty-three Eva lost her battle with cancer. Argentina's streets overflowed with mourners and flowers for the young woman who had become the "Spiritual Leader of the Nation."

Sheryl Sandberg

1969–

Technology Executive

Sheryl Sandberg is a leader of a different kind – as Chief Operating Officer of Facebook, she is empowering women in the tech industry and beyond.

After joining Facebook in 2008, Sheryl helped to make it one of the biggest websites in history. She is also now a billionaire, but Sheryl isn't all about money – she believes that, even today, not enough women hold positions of power.

Her 2010 TED talk, "Why we have too few women leaders," is devoted to women facing inequality in the workplace and has been watched over 5 million times. Her 2013 book *Lean In* encourages women to strive for the top jobs, while her Lean In Foundation helps women all over the world to dream big and aim high. In Sheryl's words, "A world where half of our countries and half of our companies were run by women would be a better world."

Laura Bush 1946-

First Lady, Teacher, Librarian

As a child growing up in Midland, Texas, Laura Bush loved nothing more than curling up on her mother's lap and listening to her read. Ever since, she has been on a mission to share her passion for reading by becoming a champion of children's literacy and education.

After earning degrees in early education and library science, Laura taught elementary school for several years before landing her dream job as a librarian. In 1977 she met future husband, George W. Bush. When he became governor of Texas in 1995, Laura was thrust into public life! As First Lady of Texas, she focused on causes close to her heart. She raised nearly $1 million for public libraries and created the First Lady's Family Literacy Initiative for Texas, which encouraged families to read together.

In 2000, when her husband was elected president of the United States and Laura became First Lady to the nation, she took her love of literacy all the way to the White House. There she created "Ready to Read, Ready to Learn," an education program that aimed to get all children reading by the time they started school. She also helped to launch the annual National Book Festival, which celebrates reading and features authors from around the world. During President Bush's second term, Laura worked hard to raise awareness for women's health across the country and beyond and, in 2007, the Laura W. Bush Institute for Women's Health at Texas Tech University was named for her.

Since leaving the White House in 2009, Laura has continued to support literacy at every turn. Each year, the Laura Bush Foundation awards about $1 million to US schools and libraries, while Laura herself inspires young people everywhere to fall in love with reading and learning for life.

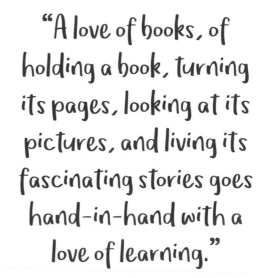

"A love of books, of holding a book, turning its pages, looking at its pictures, and living its fascinating stories goes hand-in-hand with a love of learning."

Emmeline Pankhurst 1858–1928

Women's Rights Activist

Emmeline Pankhurst was one of the most influential people of the twentieth century. At a time when women were considered inferior to men and their freedoms restricted, Emmeline led a forty-year battle to secure women's equality and the right to vote in the UK. Some countries already had voting equality, but the suffragettes' eventual victory led to emancipation in Britain and changed the course of history.

Emmeline Goulden was born in Manchester to parents who were active in politics and supported women's rights. At just fourteen, Emmeline begged to accompany her mother to a suffrage meeting, and from that moment on she was committed to the cause.

In 1879, she married Richard Pankhurst, a barrister and fellow supporter of women's equality. Over the next five years Emmeline gave birth to five children, but her passion for politics never dwindled. She and Richard believed that all women – single, married or widowed – should be allowed to vote, and in 1889 they founded the Women's Franchise League. But the group fell apart a year later. Richard died in 1897, but Emmeline's fight was far from over. Frustrated with the lack of progress in parliament through peaceful means, she vowed to take action. In 1903, she cofounded the Women's Social and Political Union (WSPU), a female-only party that employed sometimes violent tactics. Suffragettes, including Emmeline's daughters, Christabel and Sylvia, protested in their thousands. They marched through London, smashed windows and chained themselves to railings. Over 1,000 fearless suffragettes, including Emmeline, were arrested and sent to prison, where they went on a hunger strike. Guards brutally attempted to force-feed them, but this caused outrage and only encouraged support for their cause.

Not everyone agreed with Emmeline's tactics. Many considered the suffragettes "unladylike" and destructive. Millicent Fawcett, who led the more peaceful National Union of Women's Suffrage Societies, said that the violence stood in the way of progress.

But everything changed when World War I broke out. All imprisoned suffragettes were released, and Emmeline put the group's demonstrations on hold in favor of patriotism and unity.

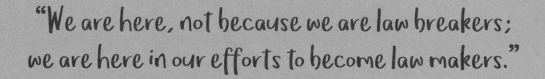

"We are here, not because we are law breakers; we are here in our efforts to become law makers."

While men were away fighting on the front lines, she campaigned for women to take over their factory and farm jobs. This proved vital to the war effort and also convinced the government to pass the 1918 Representation of the People Act, which granted women over the age of thirty voting rights, with limitations. It wasn't full suffrage – most men were allowed to vote at twenty-one – but it was a significant step.

In later life, Emmeline focused her energy on other political matters. But years of hunger strikes and struggle had taken a toll on her health. Just weeks after her death at sixty-nine, the UK parliament finally passed a bill that gave women the same voting rights as men. Emmeline and her fellow suffragettes had sacrificed everything on the long and grueling path to victory, but at last, their fight for equality had prevailed.

Eleanor Roosevelt

1884–1962

Diplomat, Activist and First Lady

Before Eleanor Roosevelt, a First Lady remained behind the scenes. But once her husband, Franklin D. Roosevelt, was elected president in 1933, Eleanor was determined to use her position to advance the causes she believed in.

At a time when equality was controversial, Eleanor campaigned fiercely for the rights of others – from women and young people to African- and Asian-Americans and World War II refugees. As the first US delegate to the United Nations, she also oversaw the creation of the Universal Declaration of Human Rights – the document that enshrines the freedoms and rights to which all human beings are entitled, and which changed the course of human history.

Angela Merkel

1954–

Politician and Chancellor

Angela Merkel is the chancellor of Germany, and she is often described as the "leader" of the European Union and the most powerful woman in the world.

When Angela was young, Germany was still split by the Berlin Wall into East and West Germany. Growing up in East Germany, Angela entered politics after the fall of the Wall in 1989, and was elected to the Bundestag, later becoming the first woman leader of the Christian Democratic Union party. In 2005, she was elected Chancellor of Germany and has been in power ever since.

Angela has faced many difficult challenges throughout her leadership, from the global financial crash to the migrant crisis. But during her time as chancellor she has remained steadfast and decisive. Under her government, Germany has grown stronger and richer, while Angela has proved she has real staying power as a leader.

Estée Lauder

1908–2004

Businesswoman and Entrepreneur

Estée Lauder is the name of a global cosmetics company, but it all began with one woman's vision.

Born to Hungarian immigrants in New York, Estée discovered she had a passion for beauty when she helped out at her uncle's cosmetics company. Starting with just four face creams, she formed Estée Lauder with her husband and soon the range grew to include makeup, hair care, skin care and fragrance.

Estée herself was an incredible salesperson and marketer – she chose the brand's characteristic turquoise packaging and created Youth-Dew, the first-ever perfumed bath oil. She also pioneered the first male toiletries brand and the now industry standard of "free gift with purchase" to promote her products.

Thanks to its founder and leader, Estée Lauder is now a multi-billion-dollar business, while Estée is celebrated as a true visionary of her time.

Indira Gandhi

1917–1984

Politician and Prime Minister

Indira Gandhi was destined to be a politician. The only daughter of India's first prime minister, Jawaharlal Nehru, she entered politics at age thirty. Just two years after her father died in 1964, Indira became the country's new leader. To date she is the only female prime minister to have governed India.

Indira was a resilient and determined leader. She improved agriculture, which solved India's long-standing food shortage. When neighboring Pakistan entered a civil war, she gave refuge to millions fleeing the area and supported the Bengali independence movement. When the Bengalis won, she helped Bangladesh to become a sovereign country.

However, some criticized Indira for her more authoritarian policies. She was imprisoned in 1978 for corruption but returned to power in 1980. Indira was assassinated in 1984. While her leadership continues to divide opinion, she remains the longest-serving female prime minister in history.

Kathleen Kennedy 1953–

Film Producer and Head of Lucasfilm

Kathleen Kennedy is considered to be the most powerful woman in Hollywood. The producer of nearly eighty movies – many of them classics, including the Back to the Future series, *Jurassic Park* and *The Goonies* – she now runs the *Star Wars* movie empire, Lucasfilm.

Kathleen studied telecommunications and film in California before securing her first job as a TV camera operator. But after seeing the sci-fi hit *Close Encounters of the Third Kind*, she was inspired to try moviemaking.

She got her big break when top director Steven Spielberg hired her as his assistant, later giving her a coproducer credit on his new film, *E.T. the Extra-Terrestrial. E.T.* was an instant smash, becoming one of the most popular sci-fi movies ever made! Since then the duo has transformed the film industry with hit after box-office hit.

But in 2012, another Hollywood mogul came calling. George Lucas was looking for someone to replace him as head of Lucasfilm, and he had one woman in mind. *Star Wars: Episodes I, II* and *III* had received bad reviews, and he needed someone to revive the franchise. Kathleen is known for big-budget movies that don't sacrifice character and here was her chance to prove the formula could work for a *Star Wars* reboot. Not only did she accept the task but *Star Wars: The Force Awakens* – the first episode with a female character as its central hero – became the most successful episode in the series!

In fact, almost everything Kathleen touches turns to box-office gold. Her projects have received 120 Oscar nominations, and she has made three of the most profitable films in history. With more *Star Wars* films to follow and multiple other projects in the pipeline, the Force is most definitely with Kathleen.

"So, do, or do not. There is no try. The Force is female."

Valentina Tereshkova

1937–

Cosmonaut, Engineer and Politician

June 16, 1963. Valentina Tereshkova straps into the Russian spacecraft *Vostok 6* and nervously awaits countdown. Moments later the capsule will blast into the atmosphere and beyond, making Valentina the first woman to enter space.

Valentina left Earth as part of an experiment to test the effects of spaceflight on the female body. Only a year earlier she'd been working in a textile factory, but she was also a keen skydiver — a skill that would stand her in good stead for her historic voyage.

Valentina went through months of training to become a cosmonaut, but she still suffered from sickness during the flight. But three days later, and having orbited Earth forty-eight times, *Vostok 6* carried her safely back home. Later she would earn a PhD in engineering and become a politician, but it was her trailblazing journey in space that rocketed Valentina into the history books.

Carolyn Porco

1953–

Planetary Scientist

When thirteen-year-old Carolyn Porco gazed through a telescope at Saturn's rings, she found her life's passion. Almost twenty-five years later, Carolyn led the Imaging Team of the Cassini-Huygens mission, which sent a spacecraft to photograph Saturn. The team discovered seven new Saturn moons, more planetary rings, and a hydrocarbon lake on Titan, Saturn's largest moon. Quite the journey for both the mission and Carolyn!

Before Cassini, Carolyn worked on Voyager 2, a decade-long exploration of our solar system. When Voyager 2 returned data from Saturn, Carolyn made several breakthroughs concerning the relationship between the planet's rings and its magnetic field. For this she received the ultimate reward: an asteroid, 7231 Porco, named in her honor.

Carolyn is now working on the New Horizons mission to Pluto and the Kuiper Belt, a mission she believes will bring us closer to solving the mysteries of our solar system.

Mary Leakey

1913–1996

Archaeologist and Paleoanthropologist

On the sweltering Serengeti Plains of Tanzania in 1959, Mary Leakey was digging an archaeological site when she spotted a bone in the ground. On closer inspection, it was part of a skull – one of the most important bones ever to be found, and the first of its kind. It belonged to *Paranthropus boisei*, an ancestor of humans dating back 1.75 million years! The "East Africa Man" is even more special because many believe he was the first hominin to use stone tools, making him an important link on the evolutionary chain between apes and humans.

Mary went on to uncover 3.75-million-year-old hominin fossils and a trail of their preserved footprints, evidence that these ancient ancestors walked upright on two legs. While at the time much of her work was credited to her husband, Mary eventually gained the respect she deserved as a true pioneer of the field.

Tu Youyou

1930–

Pharmaceutical Chemist and Educator

Tu Youyou is best known for making an extraordinary discovery that would go on to save millions of lives.

Malaria, a disease transmitted by mosquito bite, causes fever, vomiting, headaches and often death. During the 1960s, one particular strain affected thousands in tropical Southeast Asia. At the time, Tu was working at the China Academy of Traditional Chinese Medicine. She had the idea to test hundreds of herbs before learning she could extract artemisinin from sweet wormwood, a type of plant. Tests on animals, and later humans, including Tu herself, proved it worked. Artemisinin is now the standard treatment for that type of malaria.

Tu is now Chief Scientist at the same research facility where she made her historical discovery. Finally, in 2015, she became the first Chinese citizen to be awarded a Nobel Prize in Medicine.

Rosalind Franklin 1920–1958

Chemist and X-ray Crystallographer

Francis Crick and James Watson are famous for making one of the most important discoveries in history – in 1953, they solved the structure of DNA, the building block of life. But few people know that without the work of Rosalind Franklin, Crick and Watson may never have reached their pioneering conclusion.

So what exactly is DNA? Think of it as a sort of "computer code" for the human body. DNA is a very special material that tells the cells in our body what to do. It is made of long, thin molecules that carry all the information about how a living thing functions and looks. These molecules are arranged in a curving "ladder," known as a double helix. But before 1953, no one knew that DNA was the blueprint for life.

Cue Rosalind Franklin, one of the only female scientists to be working in X-ray crystallography at the time. This is the process of using X-rays to take pictures of the insides of crystals. By doing this, scientists can figure out the structure of the molecules within the crystals.

In the early 1950s, Rosalind turned her attention to DNA. She took several crystal X-ray pictures, one of which, Photo 51, showed that the DNA molecule had a spiral formation. It was this photo that led Crick and Watson to develop their groundbreaking model of the DNA molecule and its life-giving components, finally solving one of life's great mysteries.

Crick and Watson were awarded the Nobel Prize in Physiology or Medicine in 1962 for their discovery, but sadly, Rosalind had died four years earlier. It took years for her work to be recognized, but today there is little doubt of her contribution to one of science's most significant breakthroughs.

"Science and everyday life cannot and should not be separated."

Ann Bancroft

Explorer and Educator

Ann Bancroft was the first woman to conquer some of the most formidable physical challenges on the planet. In 1986, she embarked on a six-person expedition to the North Pole. Traveling with dog sleds in treacherous conditions, the team arrived at their frozen destination fifty-six days later, making Ann the first woman to reach the North Pole on foot and by sled!

The list of "firsts" continues: Ann was the first woman to cross both polar ice caps, to ski across both Greenland and Antarctica, and she led the first all-female expedition to the South Pole.

Today, the Ann Bancroft Foundation gives girls the chance to have their own adventures. Ann also uses her expeditions to teach young people about the effects of global warming on polar environments, empowering them to engage in the fight against climate change.

Maria Montessori

Educator and Doctor

At a time when many thought it impossible to educate children with learning difficulties, Maria Montessori was determined to prove them wrong. She developed pioneering materials and techniques that helped these children reach the same milestones as other children. Her methods were so successful that she tried them in the mainstream.

In her first public school, *Casa dei Bambini* (Children's House), Maria worked on her new method with fifty children. She realized that children are more motivated to learn when they are treated as individuals and have the freedom to choose their own activities. She also replaced adult-sized furniture with child-sized versions, taught life activities, such as sweeping, cooking, and caring for pets, and encouraged curiosity and creativity over grades and competition.

Today Maria's method flourishes in over 20,000 Montessori schools, inspiring children all over the world to fall in love with learning.

Radia Perlman

1951–

Inventor, Software Designer and Network Engineer

As the inventor of spanning tree protocol (STP), Radia Perlman helped to create the Internet we know today. STP is a genius solution to a tricky problem. When two or more computers within a network send messages, they compete to use the network's bridges – pathways that allow a message to be sent. This can affect the network and even stop Internet traffic altogether.

What Radia did was to invent a way for the bridges to check the messages and send them to the right place, preventing any hold-ups and clearing the way for the network to run smoothly.

Radia's ability to solve such complex puzzles earned her the nickname, "Mother of the Internet," and in 2016, she was inducted into the National Inventors Hall of Fame. Radia continues to inspire the next generation of computer-science pioneers.

Marie Curie

1867–1934

Physicist and Chemist

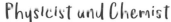

Marie Sklodowska grew up in Poland and moved to France to study science.

There she met and married Pierre Curie. Together they carried out experiments that changed the world.

When scientist Henri Becquerel discovered a strange glow coming from uranium salts, Marie and Pierre decided to experiment on the curious rays. They discovered it was the uranium atom itself generating the energy for the glow, a process that Marie named "radioactivity."

In 1903, Marie became the first woman to win a Nobel Prize in Physics for her work. Although long-term exposure to radiation made her weak, she went on to discover two new radioactive elements, polonium and radium, and also found that radiation could treat cancer. She was awarded a second Nobel Prize in 1911, in Chemistry, becoming the first person ever to win two!

Amelia Earhart 1897-1937 (disappeared)

Aviation Pioneer

Amelia Earhart always had the spirit of adventure. At a time when girls were supposed to be ladylike, she was climbing trees, hunting rats with a rifle and racing on sleds down snowy hills. But it was her first ride in an airplane at age twenty-three that changed her life. Amelia decided it was her destiny to fly.

But her journey to become a pilot would not be easy. In the 1920s women were prevented from working in the same jobs as men. But Amelia had a dream and nothing would stop her. After training as a nurse's aide, she saved $1,000 by working a variety of jobs to take her first flying lessons. Her first teacher was Neta Snook, a pioneer female aviator. Amelia bought her first airplane, a yellow Kinner Airster biplane that she called "The Canary," and flew it to an altitude of 14,000 feet, breaking the record for female pilots!

In 1928, Amelia became the first woman to fly across the Atlantic Ocean when she kept the flight log on the 20-hour 40-minute journey between Canada and Wales. Upon landing, crowds cheered for Amelia and called her the "Queen of the Air." But despite her success, Amelia noted that she had not piloted the flight that made her famous.

Amelia continued to race in flying competitions. In 1930, she set the women's speed record, flying at 181.18 miles per hour! Amelia was also one of ninety-nine female pilots to create the Ninety-Nines, an international organization that promotes and encourages women's aviation and education to this day.

While Amelia was making great strides for women, she undertook a historic journey. In 1932, she became the first woman to fly solo over the Atlantic, in just 14 hours 56 minutes. Three years and many other records later, she was also the first person to solo fly the 2,408-mile distance between Hawaii and California.

In 1937, Amelia began planning her most difficult and dangerous mission yet: a flight around the globe. To succeed, she would need to fly a grueling 29,205 miles across continents and oceans. Amelia took off from California, but she and her crew had to abandon the first attempt when their aircraft was badly

damaged. Later that year, Amelia and her flight navigator Fred Noonan started a second attempt. Departing from Miami, she made it 22,000 miles to New Guinea. On July 2, 1937, they set off to complete the remaining distance over the Pacific. But during the first leg, all radio contact was lost, and Amelia's voice disappeared from the airwaves. Despite a long search, the plane and its pilots were never found.

Amelia's life was cut short, but she became a hero. Her courage, coolness under pressure and staggering success in a male-dominated field opened the doors to generations of female aviators. To them she will always be the "Queen of the Air."

"My ambition is to have this wonderful gift produce practical results for the future of commercial flying and for the women who may want to fly tomorrow's planes."

Inge Lehmann 1888-1993

Seismologist and Geophysicist

Danish scientist Inge Lehmann is famous for making a groundbreaking discovery: the Earth has a solid inner core surrounded by a molten (heated liquid) core. Before Inge's breakthrough, most scientists believed that the entire core was molten. So how on earth did Inge work out that something hidden deep beneath our planet's surface was solid, not liquid? The answer lies in earthquakes.

Seismology is the study of earthquakes. In 1936, Inge worked at the Danish Geodetic Institute, where she studied seismic data recorded from earthquakes around the world. Earthquakes send out seismic waves, massive waves of energy that travel from the epicenter (the source of an earthquake) through Earth's layers to the surface, where we see them topple buildings, collapse bridges and turn roads to spaghetti.

Scientists knew the waves changed speed as they passed through the Earth's core, but no one understood how or what was causing it. Cue Inge, who noticed that some waves were bouncing off a boundary in the core and speeding up.

Using complex mathematical calculations, she suggested this was due to an inner core made of a different material than the outer core – in other words, the inner core was solid and not molten!

With advances in technology and better machinery to measure seismic wave speeds, scientists in the 1970s were finally able to prove Inge's theory correct. She went on to receive many honors for her discovery, and in 1971, became the first woman to win the William Bowie Medal for her outstanding contribution to geophysics. She died at 104, her earthshaking discovery having forever changed the way we understand our planet.

"You should know how many incompetent men I had to compete with—in vain."

Jane Cooke Wright

1919–2013

Cancer Researcher and Surgeon

Jane Cooke Wright was a true pioneer. Her revolutionary research into cancerous tumors led her to discover the drug methotrexate, which is the basis for chemotherapy. She was also the first doctor to test cancer drugs on human tissue rather than animal tissue, and developed treatments that help to combat both skin and breast cancer.

Jane's medical breakthroughs have saved millions of lives, and she managed all this in spite of fierce gender and racial discrimination, which she overcame with courage and determination. In 1967, Jane became the first female African-American doctor to lead a top cancer research department, at New York Medical College, and the first woman president of the New York Cancer Society. Jane finally retired in 1987, after a forty-year career that saw her completely change the face of modern medicine.

Zoe Sugg

1990–

Blogger, Vlogger, Author and YouTuber

When Zoe Sugg wrote the first post on her blog, *Zoella*, in 2009, she hoped to gain followers who liked the same things she did. But instead the "normal girl" from Wiltshire, UK, became an Internet superstar.

Zoe began filming vlogs for her YouTube channel, ranging from fashion hauls to her daily makeup routine.

By 2015, her main channel had grown to 9.9 million subscribers and over 663 million views, and it continues to gain more followers every day!

Today Zoella is a global brand. Her first novel, *Girl Online*, had the highest-ever first-week sales for a debut book, and she launched her own range of beauty products in 2014. Zoella uses her huge platform to open up to her teen fan base about her struggles with anxiety, and through her work with the UK mental health charity Mind, she inspires millions to achieve their own dreams.

Grace Murray Hopper 1906–1992

Mathematician, Computer Scientist and Military Leader

Admiral Grace Murray Hopper was one of the world's first computer programmers. She created the compiler, a revolutionary computer program that transforms source code from one computer language into another, less complex language. With her innovations, she helped shape the future of computer programming and opened doors for women to enter into scientific professions.

Grace always had a boundless curiosity. At seven, she would take apart alarm clocks to see how they worked. But rather than scold her, Grace's parents encouraged their daughter's interests. At a time when women's opportunities in education were limited, Grace broke down barriers to study math and physics, earning her PhD from Yale in 1934. She then taught math for ten years before enlisting in the US Navy. During World War II, women were encouraged to help with the war effort, and Grace finally got her chance to serve as a Navy computer scientist.

After inventing her compiler, Grace led the development of Common Business-Oriented Language (COBOL), a programming language that worked on any computer and appears in software to this day. Next she became the director of the Navy Programming Languages Group, which created standards for testing computer systems that are still in use around the world. Over a decade later she was promoted to commodore (later renamed rear admiral), and at seventy-nine, was the oldest commissioned officer in the US Navy!

"Amazing Grace," as she became known, taught computer science until her death at age eighty-five. She was buried with full military honors at Arlington National Cemetery.

"A human must turn information into intelligence... We've tended to forget that no computer will ever ask a new question."

J.K. Rowling 1965–

Author, Screenwriter and Film Producer

When Joanne Rowling had the idea for a story about a wizarding school named Hogwarts while sitting on a delayed train, little did she know that it would become the best-selling series in history. The seven Harry Potter books have since sold over 400 million copies and inspired eight blockbuster films! But Jo's success didn't come easy.

Born just outside Bristol, Jo grew up in both England and Wales. She wrote from an early age, and at just eleven years old, she finished her first novel. After earning a degree from Exeter University, Jo moved to London and worked for a charity, but she never stopped writing. When she began fleshing out the story of a young wizard named Harry, she knew she had hit on something magical. Over the next five years, Jo breathed life into the characters that would become some of the most cherished in the world.

Jo became an English teacher, moved to Edinburgh with her daughter, and continued writing every chance she could. Life as a single mother was hard, but Jo finished *Harry Potter and the Philosopher's Stone* and began the long process of finding a literary agent. After twelve rejections from publishers, the book was finally published in 1997 and won most of the children's book awards that year. Jo's life changed overnight.

She went on to write the rest of the book series, coproduce the Harry Potter films and become the most famous UK author of modern times. The adventures of Harry, Hermione and Ron continue to fire the imaginations of both children and adults around the world.

"We do not need magic to change the world, we carry all the power we need inside ourselves already."

Frida Kahlo 1907–1954

Artist

Frida Kahlo is one of the world's most iconic artists. Born in a rural village outside Mexico City to a Mexican mother and German father, her surreal paintings draw from Mexican folk art and religious imagery, and are some of the most instantly recognizable in history.

Although Frida's paintings are bold, colorful and vibrant, her work emerged from darkness. At six, she was struck down with polio, an infectious disease that causes muscle weakness, and in some cases, death. Frida's right leg grew shorter and thinner, and she was bedridden for nine months. To help Frida regain her strength, her father encouraged her to take part in sports such as soccer and wrestling, which, at the time, was highly unusual for a girl!

But at eighteen, Frida faced fresh torment when the bus she was traveling in crashed. She nearly died, and she was so badly injured that she had to abandon her dreams of pursuing higher education. But despite the trauma there was hope, for it was during her recovery that Frida turned to painting.

Frida confronted her lifelong pain through her many self-portraits. In *The Broken Column* her torso is split open, revealing a cracked column in place of a healthy spine. Her body is held together with a steel corset, like the one she wore daily for support. *The Two Fridas* depicts two versions of the artist – in one, blood spills onto her white dress from a broken heart, a symbol of the constant surgeries and heartbreak Frida endured throughout her life. But in the other, her heart is intact, portraying her strength and resilience.

Many of Frida's paintings also document her relationship with the much-older muralist Diego Rivera. Theirs was a turbulent marriage, but the two shared a passion for politics and traditional Mexican heritage. Frida wore crowns of native flowers and traditional folk dresses to express her love for her country. She also confronted her unusual looks through her paintings.

With her thick eyebrows and dark hair on her upper lip, she rejected the Western idea of beauty and never shied away from portraying her true self in her art.

During the 1930s, Frida gained widespread recognition. In 1938, she held her first solo exhibition in New York, where she proved to be a phenomenon, selling half of her exhibit paintings. Finally, in 1953, she was invited to stage her first solo exhibition in her homeland. By this point confined to bed rest, she caused a stir when she arrived by ambulance and was carried into the gallery in her four-poster bed! The exhibition was a huge success, but Frida's health continued to fail and she died the following year, at just forty-seven.

A self-taught master of her craft and a true original, Frida Kahlo will forever be celebrated as the woman who turned adversity into unforgettable art.

"I paint my own reality. The only thing I know is that I paint because I need to, and I paint whatever passes through my head without any other consideration."

Virginia Woolf

1882–1941

Author

Virginia Woolf's idyllic childhood was filled with art, literature and holidays in Cornwall. But as a young woman she lost both of her parents to illness, which left her deeply depressed. She found comfort through her writing, and the memories of her childhood form the basis of her best-loved novels.

When Virginia moved to London she met the Bloomsbury Group – artists, writers and thinkers who were part of an experimental literary movement known as modernism. Virginia's best-known novel, *To the Lighthouse*, is one of the most famous examples of modernism: in contrast to a traditional story, plot is structured loosely, and instead she focuses on the characters' emotions and innermost thoughts.

Virginia's depression later returned, and she took her own life at fifty-nine. In spite of her immense suffering, today she is celebrated as a unique voice and one of history's most lyrical and creative novelists.

Annie Leibovitz

1949–

Photographer

In her fifty-year career as a top portrait photographer Annie Leibovitz has captured images of musicians, movie stars and leaders, from the Rolling Stones and Angelina Jolie, to President Barack Obama. She was also the last person to professionally photograph musician John Lennon, just five hours before his untimely death.

What makes Annie's work so special is her connection to her subject and her use of big productions, vivid colors and striking poses. While working for the magazine *Vanity Fair* she also shot several controversial covers, including actor Demi Moore displaying her bare pregnant belly.

In 1991, Annie became the first woman to hold a solo exhibition at the National Portrait Gallery, while the Library of Congress has named her a living legend. As Annie says, "I fight to take a good photograph every single time."

Beatrix Potter 1866-1943

Author, Illustrator and Environmentalist

What was your favorite Beatrix Potter tale growing up? Was it about Peter Rabbit, Mrs. Tiggy-Winkle or Jemima Puddle-Duck? If so, you're not alone; generations of children have been brought up on these timeless family favorites!

It all started when Beatrix Potter was a child. She and her brother kept a collection of small animals, including mice, rabbits, frogs and hedgehogs. Beatrix even took her favorite rabbits on family trips to Scotland and the Lake District! There she was free to explore the countryside, and she began to draw detailed illustrations, becoming a nature expert in the process.

Beatrix also sent many handwritten letters that included her lively and imaginative watercolor paintings. It was here, in a letter to the child of her former governess, that four little rabbits – Flopsy, Mopsy, Cottontail and Peter – were born. When *The Tale of Peter Rabbit* was finally published in 1902, it became an instant bestseller. Twenty-two animal tales followed, completing the much-loved menagerie.

With the profits, Beatrix bought the now-famous Hill Top Farm, where she looked after a flock of Lake District Herdwick sheep. She also became a loyal supporter of the National Trust and purchased fifteen farms for preservation. When Beatrix died in 1943, she left most of this property to the Trust, much of which now makes up the Lake District National Park.

Today, over 2 million Beatrix Potter books are sold every year, and children all over the world are still meeting and falling in love with Peter Rabbit and his charming animal friends.

"There is something delicious about writing the first words of a story. You never quite know where they'll take you."

Lena Dunham

1986–

Actor, Writer, Producer and Director

For someone so young, Lena Dunham has achieved so much! As writer, director and star of the comedy series *Girls*, she has won two Emmys and two Golden Globes. In 2013, she was also the first woman to win the Director's Guild of America award for Outstanding Directing for a Comedy Series.

When Lena began writing *Girls* she wanted to make something she hadn't seen before – a smart and funny take on female friendships and relationships. The series explores the characters' struggles with body image, self-esteem and their transition into adulthood. *Girls* became an instant hit and an inspiration to women dealing with the issues of growing up in the social media age.

In 2015, Lena also started the influential online newsletter, *Lenny Letter*, which gives young women a platform to discuss and debate feminism and inequality. As Lena says, "I'm glad if my work can make a difference."

Judi Dench

1934–

Actor

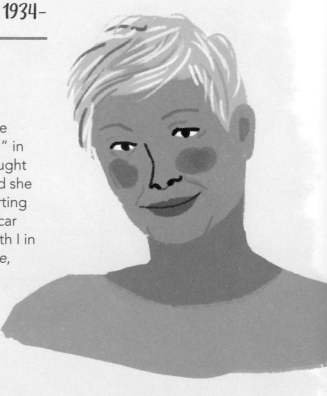

Judi Dench is arguably Britain's favorite female actor. A veteran of both stage and screen, she has achieved staggering success in her more than sixty-year career.

Judi grew up in Yorkshire and fell in love with the theater at a young age, moving to London to study at the Central School of Speech and Drama. Her first professional stage performance was as Ophelia in Shakespeare's *Hamlet*, and she went on to become one of the most-admired theater actors of her generation.

But Judi also lights up the big screen. Her role as "M" in the James Bond films brought her millions more fans, and she won both the Best Supporting Actress BAFTA and an Oscar for playing Queen Elizabeth I in 1998's *Shakespeare in Love*, despite her scenes lasting only eight minutes.

Now in her 80s and still in high demand, Judi is an inspiration to all those hoping to one day tread the boards.

Georgia O'Keeffe

1887–1986

Artist

At a time when most artists were realists, painting objects and landscapes exactly as they saw them, Georgia O'Keeffe was creating radical abstract art. Her dramatic depictions of flowers, New York skyscrapers and nature were so unusual that she was dubbed "the Mother of American Modernism." But when she traveled to the Southwest she truly found her muse. The desert landscapes of New Mexico inspired such iconic pieces as *Cow's Skull: Red, White, and Blue*, which depicts a skull floating against the vivid colors of the US flag.

Sadly, in later life, Georgia's failing eyesight forced her to stop painting, but her work is still in demand: in 2014, *Jimson Weed: White Flower No. 1* fetched $44.4 million at auction, making it the world's most expensive painting by a woman and sealing Georgia's fate as the US's most illustrious female artist.

Margaret Atwood

1939–

Author and Poet

Margaret Atwood is Canada's most celebrated writer. The author of more than forty books of fiction, poetry and essays, her award-winning work is read and revered around the world.

Margaret's most famous novel is 1985's *The Handmaid's Tale*, a story set in a nightmare futuristic world in which a dangerous and controlling regime rules, with women as its main victims. *The Handmaid's Tale* has sold in the millions, but its controversial storyline led to it being banned in some schools. However, many consider it to be one of the greatest dystopian novels of all time, and it has been translated into over forty languages. In 2017, it was also turned into a successful TV series.

Since *The Handmaid's Tale*, Margaret has written many more novels, won the Booker Prize and was inducted into Canada's Walk of Fame. Quite simply, she is considered one of the greatest and most influential writers working today.

Lady Gaga 1986-

Singer, Songwriter, Musician and Actor

Lady Gaga is a force of nature. In just ten years she has sold over 27 million albums and had a string of global Top 10 hits. Her inventive costumes and experimental performance art have made her a cultural icon, and she has empowered millions through her support for equal rights and anti-bullying campaigns.

Stefani Germanotta grew up in New York and began playing the piano at age four! By fourteen, she was writing and performing songs at open-mic nights and later studied musical theater at NYU Tisch School of the Arts. For years, she performed in New York clubs, honing the stage persona of Lady Gaga.

Gaga got her big break when she was signed to Interscope Records in 2007. The following year her debut album, *The Fame*, shot to the top of the charts and the single "Just Dance" became a worldwide smash. More hits followed with "Poker Face," "Bad Romance" and "Born This Way" – songs that showcased Gaga's originality and versatility as a singer and musician.

Gaga is also a notorious trendsetter and fashion icon. Her creative team, Haus of Gaga, is behind some of the most iconic looks in music history, from unusual makeup, headwear and footwear, to the famous "meat dress," which is now on exhibit at the Rock and Roll Hall of Fame.

Gaga also has a huge heart. Her Born This Way Foundation empowers young people to rise above bullying and tackle low self-esteem, while she is an energetic supporter of human rights. Radical and rebellious, fearless and flamboyant, Gaga's most important message to her fans is to stay true to yourself. Paws up, Little Monsters!

"Don't you ever let a soul in the world tell you that you can't be exactly who you are."

Elisabeth Lutyens
1906–1983

Classical Composer

At nine, Elisabeth Lutyens decided she would one day be a classical composer. In 1922, she went to Paris to begin her studies, before returning to London to attend the Royal College of Music. There she developed her own interpretation of the twelve-tone system, a style that gives equal importance to each of the twelve notes of the musical scale. This radical technique means that the music is often harsh-sounding, but always inventive.

Elisabeth was the first British composer to use the twelve-tone system to great effect in her concert works. She was also the first British woman to write musical scores for film and became known as the "Horror Queen" for her work on the iconic Hammer Horror movies.

Due to her unusual style, it took decades for Elisabeth to gain wider respect, but today she is remembered as one of the twentieth century's most talented and original classical composers.

Sylvia Plath
1932–1963

Author and Poet

Even as a girl, Sylvia Plath was driven to succeed. But after her father's death when she was eight, she became depressed and battled the illness for the rest of her life. She turned to poetry to help her cope, using it to examine her emotions and feelings. But while at college, Sylvia suffered a breakdown. In 1963, she wrote about the experience in her famous novel *The Bell Jar*.

After a difficult recovery, Sylvia won a scholarship to Cambridge University where she met and married the poet Ted Hughes. She continued to perfect her craft and is best known for her celebrated collections *The Colossus and Other Poems* and *Ariel*.

At just thirty, Sylvia took her own life. In 1982, she won a posthumous Pulitzer Prize for *The Collected Poems*. Her life was cut short, but Sylvia's work continues to be a gift to anyone seeking comfort.

Jaha Dukureh

1989–

Anti-FGM Activist

Jaha Dukureh was born in The Gambia, one of several countries around the world that practiced female genital mutilation (FGM). FGM is a surgery which those who practice believe protects a girl's purity and honor. In reality it is a painful and dangerous procedure, often performed by someone unqualified in surgery without pain relief. The surgery can cause infection and problems later in life, such as difficulties in childbirth. But Jaha and others have worked tirelessly to get the practice banned and criminalized.

Jaha was subjected to FGM at just one week old. As an adult she moved to the United States and started Safe Hands for Girls, an organization that educates local communities on FGM's harmful effects and works to support survivors.

Jeanne Manford

1920–2013

Schoolteacher and LGBT Activist

When schoolteacher Jeanne Manford received a call to say her gay son had been attacked, she was distraught. But when she learned the perpetrator would not be punished, she decided to act.

In the 1970s, homosexuality was still a crime in the United States. Gay people faced severe prejudice.

Jeanne wasn't about to give in to injustice: first she spoke to the media about the attack on her son. Then she and her son marched with gay protesters in New York. Back then, it was highly unusual for a parent to publicly support a gay child, and Jeanne was praised for her bravery. This encouraged her to start PFLAG, a national organization that supports the parents, friends and families of gay people. Jeanne received the 2012 Presidential Citizens Medal for her work, and today many in the LGBT community consider her a hero of their cause.

Jane Goodall 1934-

Primatologist and Conservationist

Jane Goodall fell in love with animals when she received a toy chimpanzee as a child. Since then she has dedicated her life to protecting and studying chimpanzees.

Inspired by the fictional stories of Dr. Dolittle, a vet who can "talk" with his animal patients, Jane saved up all her money from waitressing to travel from England to Africa. There she met famed archaeologist Louis Leakey. Louis was impressed with Jane's knowledge of animals and paid for her to study primatology in London.

On her return to Africa in 1960, Jane went to Gombe Stream National Park. Here she met her first family of wild chimpanzees. With her mother by her side, Jane wandered into the wild to watch the primates in their natural habitat. At first the chimps were nervous, but with persistence, Jane won them over. Sitting mere feet away from the primates for many months, Jane was able to observe chimp behaviors never seen before, such as hunting for meat, cuddling and using twigs as tools to "fish" for termites! Jane also noted that the chimps, some of whom she named, had distinct personalities.

Her observations changed the way we think about chimps, and showed us that they are more similar to humans than first thought.

Today, Jane is one of the world's leading authorities on primates, and she devotes her life to protecting them from extinction. In 1977, she opened the Jane Goodall Institute, which educates communities in methods of conservation. Now a dame and a UN Messenger of Peace, it is Jane's hope that her great-grandchildren will one day be able to see wild apes in Africa.

"The least I can do is speak out for those who cannot speak for themselves."

Nawal El Saadawi

Doctor, Writer and Equal Rights Activist

Nawal El Saadawi was taught to always speak out for what she believes. After graduating as a medical doctor from the University of Cairo in 1955, she eventually rose to become Egypt's director general of public health education from 1963 until 1972. She also worked for several years as a psychiatrist and a university lecturer.

Throughout her time in the medical profession Nawal treated many women whom she believed suffered from illness due to oppression. She went on to write about her experiences, and has since published almost 50 novels, plays and short stories on the subject of women's rights and health.

Today, Nawal's works have been translated into more than 30 languages and are taught in universities around the world. Now in her 80s, she has received a long list of international awards for her bravery and remains committed to the cause of women's equality.

Simone de Beauvoir

Writer, Philosopher and Feminist

French writer Simone de Beauvoir laid the foundations of the feminist movement. At a time when higher education had only recently become available to women, Simone studied philosophy at the Sorbonne in Paris, becoming only the ninth woman to graduate from the university. Later, while working as a teacher, she met the famous philosopher Jean Paul Sartre. They began a relationship and influenced each other's work, but never married because Simone didn't want to be distracted from working on her theories, writings and political activities.

In her most famous book, 1949's *The Second Sex*, Simone criticized the patriarchy and what she saw as women's status as second-class citizens. The book was so controversial at the time that it was banned in several places. But Simone never gave up her fight for women's equality, and today she is remembered as an icon of feminism and philosophy.

Constance Markievicz   1868-1927

Political Activist and Politician

Constance Markievicz was a revolutionary woman. Born in England to a rich family, she settled in Ireland in the early 1900s. At that time the British ruled over Ireland, and the political party Sinn Féin was fighting for Irish independence.

Despite her upper-class background, Constance had a deep concern for the poor and working classes, which spurred her into action. She fought as a soldier of the Irish Citizen Army in the Easter Rising of 1916, a six-day battle on the streets of Dublin that pitted the revolutionaries against the British Army. The rebels lost, and Constance was jailed.

A year after her release, Constance was elected to the Sinn Féin party, and she later helped to create the first Irish parliament, the Dáil Éireann. A revolutionary and politician until her death, Constance is celebrated for her brave dedication to the fight for Irish freedom.

Wangari Muta Maathai   1940-2011

Environmental and Equal Rights Activist

When Wangari Muta Maathai learned that forests all over her homeland of Kenya were being destroyed, she leaped into action. She founded the Green Belt movement, which encouraged local women to plant trees in return for a wage. In this way, she tackled two problems: women would earn money and learn new skills, and the forests would be replenished. The movement's ideals quickly spread across Africa, and today, Green Belt has planted roughly 30 million trees!

Wangari also fought for women's rights and democracy. She served on the National Council of Women of Kenya and was later elected to parliament as Assistant Minister for the Environment and Natural Resources.

In 2004, Wangari became the first African woman, and the first environmentalist, to win the Nobel Peace Prize. She is proof that with courage and commitment, anyone can plant a seed that can grow to change the world.

Mairead Corrigan Maguire 1944-

Peace Activist

In 1921, a British act of parliament split Ireland into two separate countries: the Republic of Ireland and Northern Ireland. The Republic of Ireland was mainly Catholic and had its own government. Northern Ireland was mainly Protestant and came under British rule. But many Catholics still living in Northern Ireland wished to reunite with Ireland, while the Protestants wanted to remain with the UK. The clash led to decades of violence known as the Troubles.

In the early 1970s, the fighting between Catholics and Protestants in Northern Ireland intensified. British troops were brought in to keep the peace, but this led to the streets becoming a battlefield. In 1972, the worst year of fighting, 500 people lost their lives. Many local communities became "no-go areas" and ordinary people lived in fear.

Mairead Corrigan Maguire grew up in Northern Ireland in a Roman Catholic community. As a teenager she saved up money to go to business school and eventually became a secretary. But in 1976, the violence spilled over into Mairead's life. British troops were chasing the driver of a speeding car. However, it sped out of control and ran into a mother and her three children – Mairead's sister and her young niece and nephews – and the children were killed.

Disgusted and shocked by the events, Mairead decided to act. Together with Betty Williams, a local resident who witnessed the crash, Mairead began marching for peace, with tens of thousands joining the cause. Some people opposed the marches, but Mairead and Betty wouldn't be silenced.

Eventually, the two women, along with journalist Ciaran McKeown, formed Women for Peace (later known as the Community of Peace People), a movement dedicated to finding a peaceful solution to the Troubles. They held monthly peace rallies and encouraged resolution through re-education. Within a year, the violence had dramatically reduced across the country.

By 1998, both sides were willing to lay down their weapons to discuss long-term peace. During talks, Irish and Northern Irish political parties and the British government agreed that Northern Ireland would remain a part of the UK, but that it would have its own political institutions. The UK agreed to remove its troops from the streets of Northern Ireland, and all paramilitary organizations were encouraged to hand over their weapons.

Both the people of Northern Ireland and the Republic of Ireland voted for these policies to go ahead, and the following year, power was passed to the Northern Irish Assembly. It was a historic breakthrough for the two countries.

In 1976, Mairead and Betty were awarded the Nobel Peace Prize for encouraging peace in their country. Mairead went on to become president of the Community of Peace People, and began working to promote peace in other regions affected by violence, including the Middle East. With bravery and determination, she has dedicated her life to reuniting divided communities around the world, proving that there are always alternatives to violence.

"As a pacifist I believe that violence is never justified, and there are always alternatives to force and threat of force. We must challenge the society that tells us there is no such alternative."

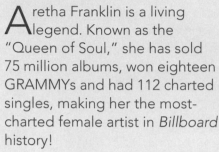

Aretha Franklin

1942–

Singer, Songwriter and Musician

Aretha Franklin is a living legend. Known as the "Queen of Soul," she has sold 75 million albums, won eighteen GRAMMYs and had 112 charted singles, making her the most-charted female artist in *Billboard* history!

Aretha was born in Memphis, "the Birthplace of Rock'n'Roll," but gospel was her first love. At fourteen she sang on her father's preaching tours, but it wasn't long before pop music came calling. Several record deals and many jazz, pop and R&B singles followed, but in 1967, she recorded the song that would catapult her to the top of the charts and into the hearts of millions. "Respect" showcased Aretha's staggering voice and made her a star.

Aretha has since won hundreds of awards, from a GRAMMY Lifetime Achievement award to the Presidential Medal of Freedom. But it is her voice – powerful, emotional, flawless – that earns her an award as one of the greatest singers of all time.

Nicola Adams

1982–

Boxer

Ringside at the 2012 London Olympics. The crowd roars as the last round of the women's flyweight boxing final gets under way. British boxer Nicola Adams dances around the ring, aiming jabs at her opponent – with a nine-point lead, all she has to do is hold on. Finally the buzzer sounds, the referee raises Nicola's gloved fist and the historic result is official: Nicola wins gold in the first-ever women's Olympic boxing championship!

Growing up in Leeds, Nicola loved watching boxing on TV with her dad. By thirteen, she had won her first bout and was on her way to becoming a champion.

After her electrifying win in London, Nicola made history again when she defended her Olympic title four years later in Rio. As the reigning Olympic, World, European and Commonwealth flyweight champion, Nicola is at the top of her game and isn't going anywhere without a fight!

Oprah Winfrey 1954–

Talk Show Host, Producer, Media Mogul, Philanthropist

In 2010, Oprah Winfrey was the only living woman to make *Life* magazine's list of 100 People Who Changed the World. She is the third richest self-made woman in North America and one of the most influential women of her generation. But her early life was one of true hardship.

Born to a teenage mother in rural Mississippi, Oprah grew up so poor that she wore dresses made from potato sacks. But she was extremely bright and won a scholarship to Tennessee State University to study communications. Later, she moved to Chicago to host *AM Chicago*. On the show, she revealed her struggles with her weight and her difficult childhood. Her warmhearted, witty and deeply personal presenting style changed the face of daytime talk shows and won her millions of viewers.

Other achievements quickly followed. Oprah started her own production company, and her TV show was shown in over 120 countries. She also launched Oprah's Book Club, which turned many previously unknown authors into overnight bestsellers! In 2011, she founded her own TV network, the Oprah Winfrey Network (OWN), which has millions of international viewers.

Despite her enormous success, Oprah has never forgotten her roots. Her charity Angel Network has raised more than $80 million, and has provided relief to the victims of Hurricane Katrina and support for girls' education in South Africa. In recognition of Oprah's work, she received the highest civilian honor, the Presidential Medal of Freedom. Oprah came from nothing, but she continues to give her all to make the world a better place.

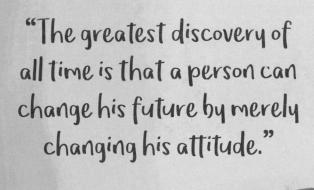

"The greatest discovery of all time is that a person can change his future by merely changing his attitude."

Serena Williams 1981–

Tennis Player

Serena Williams was just a toddler when she first picked up a tennis racket. Since then her career has been truly mind-boggling. Not only does she hold the record for the most Grand Slam singles titles of any modern player – male or female – but she has the most major titles in singles, doubles and mixed doubles combined, among active players. She has been ranked World No. 1 for six years and counting, has four Olympic gold medals and has been described as "the greatest player … that ever lived."

Serena and her older sister, Venus, both showed a talent for tennis from an early age. Recognizing that the sisters had something special, their father Richard moved the family to Florida, where the girls attended the Rick Macci Tennis Academy. Serena quickly made her mark on the junior tour, winning forty-six of her forty-nine games and ranking No. 1 in the Florida under-10s.

In 1995, Serena entered her first professional tournament. She lost that match, but two years later she started beating Top 10 players. In 1998, at the Australian Open, the Williams sisters met each other on the court for the first time in a Grand Slam tournament. Venus won that match, but the loss made Serena even more determined to succeed. Just a year later, she won her first Grand Slam title at the US Open, kicking off a run of astonishing victories.

Serena transformed the women's game. Her strength, power and attacking style allowed her to quickly overpower her opponents. Serena's forehand and double-backhand strokes are the most powerful in the women's game, while her blistering serve is the best of any female player in history. At the 2012 Wimbledon Championships, she hit a women's record of 102 aces, which was also more than any male player hit during the tournament!

While Serena dominates on the court, she is also one of the highest-paid female athletes off the court. In 2016, she earned almost $30 million through endorsements, sponsorship and prize money.

But it hasn't all been easy. Not only has Serena faced injury and burnout, but she has also dealt with surprising defeats. She credited her religious faith for reviving her inner champion, and in 2017 she won her most historic game yet: she beat her sister in the final at the Australian Open to win her twenty-third Grand Slam tournament while eight weeks pregnant! The victory saw her surpass Steffi Graf's previous record, sealing Serena's fate as one of sport's greatest-ever champions.

"Everyone's dream can come true
if you just stick to it and work hard."

Meryl Streep

1949–

Actor

During her forty-year career in film, Meryl Streep has starred in over fifty movies and is the most nominated actor – male or female – in Oscars and Golden Globes history. Meryl is known for her versatility as an actor – she is able to transform into any character, is an expert at accents and has mastered drama, comedy, tragedy and musicals. She used these gifts to great effect in her three Oscar-winning movies, *Kramer vs. Kramer* (1979), *Sophie's Choice* (1982) and *The Iron Lady* (2011).

But despite her monumental success, Meryl is no diva: she is a huge inspiration to other actors and a role model to millions.

Agatha Christie

1890–1976

Author and Playwright

Agatha Christie is known as the "Queen of Crime" for good reason – her sixty-six murder-mystery novels and fourteen short-story collections have sold an incredible 2 billion copies, making her the best-selling novelist in history.

Agatha is famous for the modern murder-mystery story: a murder is committed, there are several suspects, and the detective must work to uncover their secrets and solve the crime. At the end, the detective gathers the suspects in one room to reveal the murderer.

As well as creating Hercule Poirot and Miss Marple, two of the most famous fictional detectives of all time, Agatha also wrote the play *The Mousetrap*. Another murder mystery with a twist ending, it holds the record for the longest-running play – it opened in London in 1952 and plays to this day.

Agatha died in 1976 but her work continues to entertain fans around the world.

Björk 1965–

Singer, Songwriter and Music Producer

There is nobody quite like Björk. Ever since she landed her first record deal at age eleven, she has been on the cutting edge of music, fashion and art, and has redefined what it means to be a pop star.

Growing up in Iceland, Björk Guðmundsdóttir was destined to stand out. At a young age she learned to play piano and flute, and began composing symphonies at just six! After forming several punk-rock bands and fronting the indie band The Sugarcubes, she launched a solo career. On her first solo album, 1993's *Debut*, she experimented with pop, jazz, dance and electronica.

Despite more than twenty UK Top 40 hits, five Brit awards and a string of GRAMMY nominations, Björk has never chased mainstream popularity, preferring instead to forge her own unique path. She fused classical music with electronica on her 1997 album *Homogenic*, while in 2011, she experimented with digital technology in pop music through *Biophilia*, the first album to include interactive apps for each of its songs.

With each new album, Björk showcases her one-of-a-kind voice and talent for music production. A true original and an inspiration to millions of fans, the world would be a very boring place without her!

"It would be flattering to be thought of as somebody who celebrated life."

Coco Chanel

1883–1971

Fashion Designer and Businesswoman

Today Chanel is known as a global fashion empire, but it all began with just one woman. When her mother died of bronchitis, twelve-year-old Gabrielle "Coco" Chanel was sent to an orphanage. It was a stark change but a blessing in disguise because it was here that Coco learned to sew.

Later she worked as a seamstress and created her first line of sports-casual garments. Gone were the fussy corsets of previous generations – working women needed practical yet sophisticated clothes that moved freely, and Coco made them! She designed the jersey dress, the tweed skirt-suit and the little black dress, revolutionary designs that women wear to this day.

In 1921, Coco opened a Paris boutique where she introduced new lines of accessories, jewelry and perfume. It was here that the timeless Chanel No. 5 fragrance was born, sealing Coco's fate as one of history's most iconic designers.

Florence Griffith Joyner

1959–1998

Track and Field Athlete

Florence Griffith Joyner is the fastest woman runner in history. In 1988, she ran the fastest-ever times in both the women's 100m and 200m, records that still stand to this day.

Going into the 1988 Seoul Olympics, Florence – known as "Flo-Jo" to her fans – was the favorite to win both of her sprint events. But not only did she win, she practically flew across the line! In the US team trials, she ran the 100m in a blistering 10.49 seconds. During the 200m Olympic final itself, Flo-Jo did it again, finishing in an unbelievable 21.34 seconds! No woman has ever come close to running that fast since.

Later, injury put an end to Flo-Jo's dreams of a comeback, and at just thirty-eight, she died in her sleep. A true champion, she will always be remembered for creating two of the most memorable moments in Olympic history.

Joni Mitchell 1943–

Singer, Songwriter, Musician and Painter

Joni Mitchell is one of the most influential songwriters of all time. During a career spanning over forty years, she has bared her soul through her personal lyrics, developing a confessional style of songwriting that defined a generation.

Roberta Joan Anderson was born in Fort Macleod, a tiny town in the vast, open space of the Canadian prairies. At nine she contracted polio, and it was during her recovery that Joni taught herself to play guitar. She adapted the tuning to suit her polio-weakened fingers, a tool she later used to magical effect in her highly original melodies. After finding art school too restrictive, she dropped out to follow her dream of becoming a musician and quickly made a name for herself on the folk scene.

When Joni's marriage to fellow folk singer Chuck Mitchell failed, she fled to Los Angeles, where, in 1968, she released her debut album, *Song to a Seagull*. But it was 1971's *Blue* that made Joni a star. The album was an artistic masterpiece, showcasing her crystal-clear voice, melancholy chords and powerfully poetic lyrics.

Several of her songs, including "Big Yellow Taxi" and

"Woodstock," became anthems.

By the mid-1970s, Joni was in experimental mode, fusing free jazz with pop across a range of instruments. Her 1974 album, *Court and Spark*, was her biggest hit to date, while the sophisticated sound, compositions and musical arrangements of 1976's *Hejira* established Joni as a fearless artist.

Since then, Joni's genius has captivated generations of fans, and in 2002, she was honored with the GRAMMY Lifetime Achievement award. With an emotional range and depth that sets her apart from her peers, she has proven herself unafraid to sacrifice sales in the pursuit of her unique creative vision.

"I'm a very analytical person, a somewhat introspective person; that's the nature of the work I do."

Tavi Gevinson

Writer, Editor and Actor

Tavi Gevinson was just eleven when she started her blog, *Style Rookie*. Through it, she showcased her quirky personal style in funny and intelligent posts. *Style Rookie* and Tavi stood out – she quickly became famous for her articulate writing and her knowledge of fashion. Soon she was being invited to attend the world's top catwalk shows and style photo shoots.

In 2011, at only fifteen, Tavi founded *Rookie* online magazine. *Rookie* is unique, as it is mainly written by teenage girls and focuses on issues affecting them, such as body image, relationships and growing up in the social media age.

Today Tavi's influence shows no sign of stopping – she was a speaker at TEDxTeen, has acted in several films and is considered a feminist role model to millions of young women around the world.

Laura Dekker

Sailor

Imagine the scene: you're about to set sail around the world on a 12m Ketch boat. It will be two years before you return to land. Your journey will test you physically and mentally. And did we mention you'll be doing it alone? Sounds like an impossible feat? Not for Laura Dekker, who at sixteen became the youngest-ever person to circumnavigate the globe single-handed.

Laura has sailing in her blood – she spent her early life at sea with her parents, and for her sixth birthday received her first boat, *Guppy*. After several shorter solo journeys, Laura decided to take on the ultimate challenge: a solo circumnavigation. On August 21, 2010, she set off from Gibraltar – 5,600 nautical miles later, Laura arrived back safe and landed in the record books.

Now in her twenties, Laura lives on a boat and is dreaming up her next sailing adventure!

Simone Biles 1997–

Gymnast

Day eleven at the 2016 Rio Olympic Games. The stands in the Arena Olímpica do Rio are packed in anticipation for one of the Games' most thrilling events: the women's gymnastics floor final. As Simone Biles takes to the floor and extends a single graceful arm to the ceiling, there are cheers from the crowd. The driving beat of the music erupts, and Simone explodes into action.

Simone Biles had a difficult start in life. Born in Ohio to a mother who struggled with substance abuse and an absent father, Simone was in and out of foster care as a child. Later her grandparents adopted her, and Simone settled into life in Texas. She first tried gymnastics at age six and grew to adore the sport that would make her a star.

In 2013 Simone became the first African-American to win gold in the World Championships all-around event. Around this time, she also developed her signature move – a double layout with a half-twist tumble.

During the Rio Olympics gymnastic floor event, Simone performed this move – known as "The Biles" – on the biggest stage of all. Having already won three golds in Rio, Simone landed the complex tumble and completed her floor routine without a single mistake. Moments later, the judges revealed her score: 15.966. A fourth gold was hers! Simone set the US record for most gold medals in women's gymnastics at a single Olympics. Her sheer dedication, strength and grace have made her a once-in-a-lifetime gymnast and one of the greatest athletes in history.

"We can push ourselves further. We always have more to give."

Anne Frank 1929-1945

Diarist

In 1933, when Adolf Hitler and the Nazis came to power in Germany, life for Jewish people changed overnight. Hitler viewed Jews as enemies of the state and restricted their freedoms. He stripped them of their citizenship and forced them into ghettos. Soon they were sent to concentration camps to face almost certain death in the gas chambers.

Anne Frank was an ordinary Jewish girl living an ordinary life. She and her family had moved from Germany to the Netherlands. But when Nazi tanks rolled across the border, the Franks were forced into hiding. They spent the next two years trapped in a three-story space above her father's business, relying on trusted friends to supply them with food and news of the outside world. A bookcase concealed the door to the "Secret Annex."

Stuck in the Annex, Anne kept a diary to occupy herself. Much like any other young girl's diary, it contained her hopes, fears and frustrations. But there was one huge difference: it was written under extraordinary circumstances.

On August 4, 1944, German police stormed the Annex, and the group was deported to several concentration camps. The men and women were separated. Anne never saw her father again. She died from starvation and disease at the Bergen-Belsen concentration camp, months before the war's end. She was just fifteen.

Only 5,200 of the 107,000 Jews deported from the Netherlands survived. Otto Frank was one of them. After learning that his entire family had died in the camps, he published Anne's diary as a testament to her desire to become an author. Through her writing Anne became a hero, and a voice for the millions who lost their lives in the Holocaust.

> "I still believe, in spite of everything, that people are truly good at heart."

Kiara Nirghin

2000–

Inventor

Is it impossible for a schoolgirl to change the world? Sixteen-year-old Kiara Nirghin is doing just that. When Kiara learned that her homeland, South Africa, was experiencing one of the worst droughts in its history, causing crops to die and families to go hungry, she wanted to help.

After six weeks of trial and error, the young scientist discovered that the solution lay in her kitchen! Combined and heated, orange and avocado peels make a super-absorbent polymer (SAP) – a spongelike material that stores water, which can be used to feed crops. Better still, Kiara's SAP uses cheap recycled and biodegradable materials.

Kiara's invention won the $50,000 grand prize at the 2016 Google Science Fair. She is now working with a Google mentor to test "No More Thirsty Crops" in the field and hopes it will save millions of lives.

Ellie Simmonds

1994–

Swimmer

Ellie Simmonds dreamed of competing for her country as a swimmer. And she didn't let being born with achondroplasia, or dwarfism, stop her.

At the 2008 Beijing Paralympics, Ellie won the 400m freestyle in record-breaking time, becoming the youngest member of Team GB to win an Olympic gold medal, at just thirteen.

In the 2012 London Paralympics, Ellie won gold in the 400m freestyle and 200m individual medley.

Four years later in Rio, Ellie defended her 200m individual medley title in yet another record-breaking performance. When she was awarded an MBE for her services to Paralympic sport in 2009, she was the youngest-ever person to receive the honor. Ellie continues to dominate her sport, balancing charity work with training.

Malala Yousafzai 1997–

Education Activist

Fifteen-year-old Malala Yousafzai was traveling home on a school bus in Pakistan when her life changed forever. A gunman flagged the driver down, boarded the bus and shot the schoolgirl. The bullet passed through her head and neck, lodging in her shoulder, but she miraculously survived the assassination attempt. Malala's crime? She had spoken out against women's oppression in her fight to secure education for all.

Malala was born in Swat District, northwest Pakistan. An exceptional student, she didn't think it was fair that her brothers had futures full of opportunities, while she and other girls could only see a life in the home. She decided the only way to change this was to empower herself through education.

But when the Taliban seized Swat District, everything changed. They restricted women's rights and stopped girls from attending school. Malala made it her mission to speak out against the terrible treatment. It would have been a brave and bold step for anyone, but Malala was just eleven!

Soon the BBC Urdu website asked the schoolgirl to blog about life in Swat District. It was a brave undertaking, but despite the risks, Malala was ready to share her experiences. She handwrote posts under the name "Gul Makai" before a reporter emailed them to the BBC. Her message was heard around the world, but it meant she became a target.

After more fighting in the region, a peace deal was declared. The ban on girls attending school was lifted, and Malala returned to class to study for her exams. Yet the town's future was still uncertain. The Pakistani Army moved in to drive out the Taliban. Malala stepped up her protests, appearing in a documentary and on national TV stations. This meant she was no longer anonymous. She received threats for speaking out, but didn't allow the fear to silence her.

Then, after taking an exam on October 9, 2012, Malala was shot on her way home. She was airlifted to a military hospital, where she had several operations to save her life, and was later moved to the Queen Elizabeth Hospital in the UK for further treatment.

The attack sparked mass protests. In support of Malala, 2 million people signed a petition that led to the first Right to Education Bill in Pakistan. World leaders praised her bravery, and after she recovered, she was invited to speak at the United Nations on her sixteenth birthday in an event called "Malala Day." Two years later, almost to the day of the attack, Malala became corecipient of the 2014 Nobel Peace Prize, the youngest-ever Nobel prize-winner, and in 2017, the youngest-ever UN Messenger of Peace.

Today Malala continues to fight for education rights. But despite her busy life, she still found time to pass her exams and earn a place at Oxford University, proving that education is the most powerful weapon of all.

"I don't want to be remembered as the girl who was shot. I want to be remembered as the girl who stood up."

You!

Inventor? Politician? Musician? Scientist? Writer?

This book celebrates women from all walks of life. With passion, curiosity and determination, these women broke down barriers, were pioneers of change, traveled to space and back, and inspired millions around the world. From the innovators and trailblazers who changed the course of history, to the heroes, champions and superstars of the future, women continue to make an unforgettable mark on the world.

You may think that to follow in their footsteps is a tall order. But each of these women was once a young girl just like you, with the same dreams, hopes and fears. Many of them faced obstacles to success, such as illness, prejudice, war and oppression, yet they persevered and prevailed against the odds. Some did not receive the recognition they deserved during their lifetime, but their belief in their abilities never faltered – they forged ahead, regardless of fame or fortune.

Whether you have a talent for math or writing, singing or science, are drawn to caring for others, animals or the environment, or find strength through leadership, there is a fearless female role model to show you the way.

So could you be the next Radia Perlman or Lady Gaga? Maybe you aspire to the success of Georgia O'Keeffe or Tu Youyou? Perhaps you yearn for adventure, like Amelia Earhart and Junko Tabei? Whatever your goal in life, and in whatever form you choose to pursue it, we can all learn one simple lesson from these women: never be afraid to be your true self. Because, as each of these women has proved to great effect, you never know… one day, it could be your turn to inspire the next generation of fantastic females.

Glossary

activist person who campaigns political or social change

assassination murder of a famous person or leader

authoritarian government or policies that force citizens to obey strict rules and give up personal freedoms

autism condition that affects a person's communication or behavior and how they relate to the world

barrister in the UK, type of lawyer who is qualified to argue cases in both the higher and lower courts

Billboard chart music industry chart that records sales of singles and albums in the US

biodegradable able to decay naturally in a way that is not harmful to the environment or people

blueprint a way of describing DNA, a type of map of a living organism's genes

boycott refuse to use a company's or organization's services or buy a product as a form of protest

box office how much money a film or play makes based on ticket sales

Braille form of written language for blind people, in which characters are formed by raised bumps that are felt with the fingertips

Bundestag German parliament; its members propose, debate and set laws

capitalism economic and political system in which private individuals own and run businesses and the production of goods

Capitol Building home of the US Congress, the chief law-making body of the US; the Capitol Building is in Washington, D.C., the US's capital city

censorship banning of certain speech, writings or parts in films that some consider inappropriate or damaging

Chancellor head of government in Germany, similar to a prime minister

chemotherapy type of cancer treatment

Civil Rights movement struggle by African-Americans in the 1950s and 1960s to achieve the same rights as white Americans, such as housing, education and the right to vote

commissioned officer senior member of the armed forces who has the authority to act on behalf of a country's leader

Commonwealth group of fifty-two nations, many of which were once part of the British Empire; Queen Elizabeth II is the Head of the Commonwealth

communism type of economic and political system in which the state owns and runs all businesses and the production of goods

compassion concern for the suffering of others

concentration camp place where large numbers of prisoners of war or persecuted civilians, such as the Jews during World War II (1939–1945), are held against their will

Congressional Gold Medal alongside the Presidential Medal of Freedom, the highest honor given to ordinary citizens in the US for an achievement that has a long-lasting impact on American history and culture

conservationist person who works to protect and preserve the environment and wildlife

constitution set of principles and laws that determine the way a country or society is governed

controversial something that leads to lots of disagreement or debate

convent home for nuns, who live together as a community and practice a religious way of life

coronation ceremony for crowning a new king or queen

corruption illegal or dishonest behavior, usually of someone in power

cosmonaut Russian astronaut

debut first time a person does something in public, such as perform or launch a book or album

democracy type of government in which citizens elect leaders through majority rule

desegregation ending laws that separate people, usually based on their race

dystopia imagined place or society in which everything is bad or cruel

electoral vote a vote cast by a member of each state's electoral college in a presidential election;

electoral college votes decide who the next president and vice president will be

emancipation freeing a person from another person's control or power; women's emancipation gave women the same rights as men, including the right to vote

empower give someone the confidence to have more power or control over their own life

entrepreneur someone who sets up their own business or multiple businesses

environmental movement political movement that aims to protect and preserve the environment (also known as the "green" movement)

equality being equal or having the same rights as others, especially in relation to work, education and the right to vote

feminism movement that fights for women's rights and equality with men

First Lady title given to a president's wife, or to the wife of a US state governor

flyweight boxer who is in the lightest weight group; boxers fight only other boxers in the same weight group

formidable impressively large, powerful or capable

founder person who starts an institution, organization or business

franchise series that is usually set in the same universe, or includes the same characters

French Resistance secret movement that fought against the Nazi occupation of France during World War II (1939–1945)

geophysics type of science devoted to the study of the Earth's processes and physical properties

Gestapo Secret State Police force in Nazi Germany (1933–1945)

ghetto during World War II (1939–1945), an enclosed section of a city under Nazi rule in which Jews were forced to live

global financial crash worldwide time of economic difficulty

global warming gradual increase in Earth's temperature caused by pollution

Great Depression worst economic downturn in modern history; it began in 1929 when the US's stock market crashed, and ended in 1939

hominin ancient ancestor of humans

humanitarian someone who is involved in improving people's lives and reducing their suffering

lie in state when a body, usually of a famous or important person, is placed in public view before it is buried

LGBT lesbian, gay, bisexual and transgender

lynching when a crowd of people punishes a person they believe to be guilty of a crime by hanging the person without a trial

missionary person who is sent to a foreign country to teach their religion to the people living there

mogul important person who is very rich and powerful

muse something, usually a person, idea or landscape, that inspires an artist's creativity

nationalism having loyal or patriotic feelings for one's country

National Trust organization in the UK that preserves and protects historic buildings and landscapes

Nobel Prizes set of annual awards recognizing extraordinary achievement in various fields, including science, literature and culture

oppression cruel or unfair treatment of a group of people, which restricts that group's rights and freedoms

paramilitary group that is organized like an army but is not an official army and is often illegal

patriarchy system of society or government in which men hold all or most of the power

persona role or character adopted by a performer

personal best best time or score ever achieved by a sportsperson in their event

pesticide substance that is used to control or kill pests, especially on crops or animals

philosophy study of ideas about knowledge, truth and existence

pioneer be the first to do something or use a new method or invention

polio infectious disease that causes muscle weakness and, in some cases, death

popular vote in the US, votes cast by citizens in a presidential election; the winner of the popular vote may end up losing the election if they lose the electoral vote

posthumous happening after a person's death, for example, a posthumous award is an award given to a person after he/she dies

Presidential Citizens' Medal second-highest award given to ordinary citizens in the US for exceptional deeds or services to the country

Presidential Medal of Freedom alongside the Congressional Gold Medal, the highest honor given to ordinary citizens in the US for outstanding contributions to national security, world peace or culture

prevail gain victory after a long struggle

primatologist scientist who studies primates (humans, great apes, monkeys and lemurs)

Pulitzer Prize award for achievement in American literature, journalism or music

resilience ability to recover from difficult conditions

revolutionary person fighting for drastic political change

Russian Revolution collective name for two revolutions in Russia, the first of which (in March 1917) overthrew the Russian Emperor's government and the second (in October 1917) in which the communist Bolshevik party took power

segregation system that keeps people of different races apart, for example, in separate schools, churches, or areas in a town or city

sovereign state or country that is independent and is not subject to the authority of another state or country

stereotype simplified idea of the characteristics of a certain group of people

subservient obeying the orders of another person, group or government without question

suffragette woman campaigning for the right to vote through organized protest

surreal seeming like a dream or fantasy; not real

TED Talk/TEDxTeen short lectures on a huge range of subjects, from culture to science, which can be watched online. TED stands for Technology, Entertainment and Design, while exceptional teens give TEDxTeen talks

trade union organization of workers in a particular trade that is formed to protect the workers' rights

trailblazer person who is the first to do something, paving the way for others to follow

turbulent not stable or calm

UNICEF Goodwill Ambassador person who is chosen to represent the United Nations International Children's Emergency Fund (UNICEF), an organization that provides assistance and emergency food and healthcare to children and mothers in developing countries

United Nations global organization formed in 1945, at the end of World War II, to promote peace, human rights, and political and economic cooperation among its member countries

UN Messenger of Peace person from fields of art, literature, entertainment, science, sports or other fields of public life, chosen to promote the UN's work around the world

virtuoso person who is extremely good at something and well-known for their talent

visionary person with original and creative ideas about what the future could be like

vlog short video that a person uploads to the Internet to broadcast their opinions or thoughts on a subject